PERSPECTIVES IN READING

PERSPECTIVES ON READING

A SYMPOSIUM ON THE THEORY AND TEACHING OF READING

EDITED BY DESMOND SWAN

THE GLENDALE PRESS

ISBN 0 907606 03 2

Published by
The Glendale Press
18 Sharavogue, Glenageary Rd. Upr.,
Dun Laoghaire, Co. Dublin.

Typeset by Print Prep Ltd.

Printed by Uniprint

CONTENTS

FOREWORD

Reading is a complex, relational process. Its meaning resides in the interaction between the reader and the matter read, while at the same time the art or process of reading has some universal aspects. No doubt deriving from its complexity, a fragmentation has occurred in recent decades in the study of reading, which has produced some strange results. Fruitful though it is, this fragmentation has led to the dissection of what is a unified, organic activity among several disciplines that have become strangers to each other. This collection of papers rests on the assumption that none of these disciplines has a monopoly of understanding of the reading process, that the separation of process from product can be misleading in this context, and above all, that the teacher cannot afford to ignore any major aspect of the process itself. The papers presented here, while dealing with several aspects of reading, all share a common concern for the better understanding and the improved teaching of reading.

As with the field of education in general, the study of reading in recent decades has tended to be dominated by empirical scientists, notably psychologists and psycholinguists, resulting in a strongly analytical approach. Analyses of reading itself, based on current experimental models and theories, are well represented in this volume, especially in the section entitled *Studies of the Reading Process*. The work of Goodman provides the stimulus for the papers by Farren and by Ryan. But of course further light is shed on the process of reading in many papers which analyse it in other terms.

Analyses by means of standardised tests and other measurement instruments are also important. It is, after all, now incumbent on teachers to possess this language of numbers, so as to know how to use it without being mesmerised by it. But if the technology of standardised measurement is part of the teacher's stock-in-trade, his knowledge must encompass an awareness of the weaknesses inherent in it as well. In his paper, McBride exposes with meticulous care one frequently ignored shortcoming in the use of standardised reading tests.

Reading is virtually inseparable from formal learning at school, and a central consideration here will be the learning of reading itself. This has a section of the book to itself, with a mixture of emphases, both empirical and pedagogical, and an examination of the correlates of failure as well as success.

Complementing this is the section on *The Teaching of Reading.* In a broad sense the *raison d'etre* of the conference at which this collection of papers was presented, was the pedagogy of reading. The focus here ranges from the junior school through the secondary school and on to the teacher-training level. Since the United States and Scotland have in so many ways pioneered both theory and practice in this field, it is fitting that papers from both these countries should figure prominently here. In particular, Livingstone's paper usefully sums up the debate on the nature of reading comprehension, and draws its implications for the teacher.

Adult literacy teaching differs radically as between Western countries and developing countries. In the latter kind of society not only may the book possess magical powers, it may also encompass the law itself. There are few, if any, English-speaking countries where universal education has wrought universal literacy, and we in Ireland have only recently begun working to help the considerable number of adults who are illiterate in our society. On the other hand, literacy is not achieved in developing countries without paying a certain price, as John and Miriam Dean point out in their paper which is based on work in the Third World.

Reading is of course a two-way process. "I have been read by Eliot's poems and by Ulysses for a good many years now," W.H. Auden once remarked. "Some of these books at first rejected me; I bored them. But as I grew older and they knew me better, they came to have more sympathy with me."

The sympathy and experience that literature can engender in the reader, if it is but patient enough with him, and he in turn with it, are sensitively elucidated here by the poet Seamus Heaney. Of course, these qualities of reading may elude the technology of those of us who measure and quantify; their action on the mind and the imagination is, as Heaney points out, unquantifiable. All the more important therefore is it to present the creative writer's view of reading. Neither can the teacher of reading at any level afford to ignore the lessons that history teaches us about what we teach children to read in schools. Hence the decision also to include papers on historical studies of reading, in the colonial American and the post-colonial Irish elementary schools.

The papers presented here constitute both an attempt to illuminate the very great diversity of the scholarly interests that converge in reading, and a move towards re-introducing their practitioners to each other. These twin aims inspired the organisers of the conference at which they were presented. The Editor is indebted to the Reading Association of Ireland for permission to publish them, and above all to the authors of the papers for their contribution to the multi-disciplinary study of reading presented here. He also gratefully acknowledges the financial help of UNESCO towards their publication.

For the convenience of the reader, the usage of English has been standardised throughout the book.

It should be noted that the institutional affilation given for each author is that which applied at the time of presenting the paper, unless otherwise stated.

DESMOND SWAN
University College, Dublin

1. THE TEACHING OF READING

1. Reading in the Secondary School – Taught or Caught?

Desmond Swan, University College Dublin

"Reading is not a generalised skill that, once developed in an English class, can be applied in a special field. Rather, reading involves the ability to interpret this or that particular area of experience. Basic instruction, no matter how excellent, is not enough. Reading abilities must be developed in the areas where they are to be used."[1]

Growth in reading ability is usually a continuous and cumulative, though irregular, process. Once commenced it may well continue, under favourable conditions, not only throughout childhood and adolescence, but even during adulthood itself. True, its growth is greatest during the primary school years, but if growth in reading ability were to cease on transition to the secondary stage, then most secondary schooling would itself be impossible.

There is, nevertheless, a widespread assumption among second-level school teachers, that teaching reading is none of their business, or that if it is, it is confined to the remedial level alone. This paper rejects any such assumption. It proposes rather that while the basic skills of reading will have been mastered by the great majority of children in the primary school, nevertheless there are further identifiable skills and related attitudes, feelings and habits, which can only be inculcated, even in the average or the highly competent reader, at the secondary stage of schooling. It goes on to identify the precise nature of the teacher's responsibility in this regard, beginning with the stage of transfer from the primary school.

Reading at the Transition Stage

The transition from primary to post-primary school, especially when it involves a change of location, as well as new teachers and classmates, is now often seen as a critical juncture, a fragile bridge which may be marked by a slowing down or even a regression in some pupils' reading growth.[2, 3] Where it does occur however this lapse is usually a temporary one.

Different explanations of the regression are offered. Artley[3] attributes it to the discontinuance of explicit reading instruction beyond this point. Dearborn and Rothney[4] had found that a generally slower rate of overall mental growth set in from age 10 onward, while Lenneberg[5] adduced evidence that the twelfth year marks the end of a critical phase in language acquisition as a whole, which no doubt could have a direct impact on learning to read.

Wall[6] on the other hand felt it probable that no child meets the 'impersonal kaleidoscope' of the whole succession of new subjects and teachers, which the child encounters for the first time on transferring into the secondary school, without experiencing some temporary strain at least. Besides, for the very weak reader, there will be the daily apprehension about his problem being freshly exposed to new teachers or classmates. Schonell[7] indeed spoke of a 'decision to fail' or a sort of educational capitulation which sets in at about age 10 to 11 in those pupils who have been allowed to drift and have experienced continued failure in the "three R's", despite the capacity to achieve at higher levels than they do. Whatever the cause then, there is reason to feel that far from ignoring the teaching of reading at this stage, the secondary school needs to adopt an explicit and coherent policy of teaching reading as part of the teaching of each subject, as well as constituting a precaution against transitory problems becoming more deep-seated through lack of attention.

A commonly heard argument against doing so seems to derive from the assumption that all pupils will have reached a uniform minimum standard of reading achievement by the time they leave the primary school. In fact the research evidence fails to support any such assumption. Young[8] found the range of levels among seventh grade pupils in Alberta to stretch from below grade four to above grade eleven, or in Irish equivalents, from below fourth class primary up to about fifth year secondary. Sheldon[9] supported this, while Foster[10] reported a similar finding. In a national survey, the present writer found the literacy levels of a representative sample (n = 3,377) of first year pupils in Irish post-primary schools to range from the equivalent of the average 7 year-old in the weakest, up to the average adult level among the best.[11] Of course it is no more to be expected that all pupils, on leaving the primary school will have reached the same level of achievement in anything, than that all who start a race together will reach the finishing line at the same time.

Teaching Reading in the Secondary School

The teaching of virtually every subject on the post-primary curriculum depends so heavily on the written word – whether in worksheets, on the blackboard, in pupils' notebooks, in the text-book or in other reference materials, that it is almost taken for granted. There is good reason to believe, however, that unrecognised reading difficulties rather than low general intelligence may sometimes be the real obstacle to a pupil's progress in any of these subjects. The teacher needs therefore to reach an accurate estimate of the pupil's present reading ability, relevant to the subject in question, as a separate teaching task, and to build on this in ways that are appropriate to the pupil's current level of intellectual maturity, to his present purposes and interests and, of course, to the nature of the subject in question. The secondary teacher's responsibility here is frequently conceptualised for convenience as occurring on three levels – the developmental, the corrective and the remedial, and while these may overlap, a theoretical distinction can be maintained between them.

The corrective teaching of reading aims at adjusting the level and pace of teaching in such a way as to correct minor difficulties that arise, thus preventing a more serious lag developing. Remedial teaching addresses itself to overcoming major difficulties which have arisen and are now likely to be both cumulative and pervasive in their effects. These two levels merit further discussion in their own right[12] but the remainder of this paper deals with the developmental teaching of reading only.

Developmental Reading

At the developmental level the stress will be mainly on reading as a thinking process, or as a means to learning how to think logically, critically and creatively. The pupil needs to be led to realise the relationship between enjoyment and purpose on the one hand, and effort on the other; to question the text, rather than passively accept the authority of the writer; to bring an appropriate conceptual framework to bear on the written words, enabling them to speak to his own personal experience and at the same time enabling him to resonate with both the beauty of the words in the literature lesson and with their meaning in every lesson. In short, the teaching of developmental reading shares the highest aims of education itself, since the further development of his reading skills must facilitate the growing autonomy of the pupil as an independent learner.

Purpose is a major determinant of both speed and efficiency in reading. The specific purpose of each reading assignment should be identified and made explicit to the student – beyond such implicit ones as 'covering' a set course or passing a forthcoming examination. A large part of the teacher's task therefore will be to ensure that the student in turn realises and accepts the precise purpose of every such assignment; anything less will fail to evoke in him the effort necessary to question the material himself and grapple with new terms or knit together partial understandings, so as to comprehend adequately and respond appropriately to the text.

Purpose derives from meaning. But meaning itself, far from being something totally inherent in the text, is in fact whatever the reader constructs out of his own experience in response to it. In reading, as in every other area of learning and experience, it is ultimately personal meanings that count. Naturally, one hopes that the personal meanings which are constructed by the reader will correspond closely to those intended by the writer. But this hope is far from what actually happens in many cases and it is this gap that the teacher must be constantly aware of as the zone of potential and necessary learning. Of course we do learn from partly understood material, nor can we always ensure that the reader fully understands everything he attempts to read. Nevertheless, since repeated encounters with intractable text can certainly sap the motivation to try further, the teacher should ensure that inadequate preparation of the pupil for the reading tasks he must do, does not itself constitute an obstacle to learning.

The sheer diversity and volume of the secondary pupil's total reading tasks can be daunting in themselves. In the course of a single morning for instance the same Intermediate Certificate pupil might in a recent year have moved from Byron's "The Isles of Greece" through "Bodach an Chóta Lachtna", on to Collinear and Non-collinear Couples, and ending up with the use of quadrats, transects, valence analysis and cover abundance. No doubt, the readability of any given assignment may be roughly gauged by the teacher beforehand. But since each teacher here is a specialist, teaching the subject 'from inside' itself so to speak, he may find it difficult to appreciate the problems of someone whose view of it is still that of an outsider trying to peer in through words that often constitute a cloud of unknowing. It may not therefore be the arcane language of any individual subject that baffles the learner so much as the cumulative deficits that result from inability to 'change gears' fast enough in the course of a morning, eventually resulting in a generalised feeling of failure to cope with the written text itself. Hence the need to prepare the pupil thoroughly for the reading element in each individual assignment.

The Reading Process

Viewing reading then, in broad terms, as the recognition of, reaction to, and application of the meaning derived from written symbols, it may be analysed into several elements or sub-skills ranging from the perceptual to the cognitive and affective, as follows:

1. *Word Recognition*

This is essential to all reading. In this process we may use both visual and non-visual information.[12] The former includes all the visual characteristics of the written material, the latter referring, for instance, to structural or contextual clues. Thus in the case of the word 'zoology', the fact that the word breaks down into two parts, each one recognisable as part of the language, may be a sufficient structural clue to enable the reader to recognise it correctly.

The correct recognition of written symbols in the first place must be a major element in learning both Mathematics and Science. Failure to do so could well provide a clue to problems in logarithms and indices for instance, or even in fractions. Sometimes it is only by translating the numerical symbols into written verbal symbols that the weak pupil will recognise the nature of a problem correctly. Of course Mathematics learning at all levels is plagued by problems of inconsistent notation which however transparent to the bright, can be 'the last straw' for the weak pupil. Much of this failure at the level of symbol recognition applies to Science and Mathematical Geography as well, and the possibility of an 'allergy' to Mathematics being carried over by a pupil to new subjects such as these cannot be overlooked.

Interference of similar written symbols with each other (e.g. in Chemistry) is a problem which calls for discrimination teaching and frequent practice, but not divorced from correct association and context clues.

2. *Association*

Associating the correct meaning with the written symbol. As with language learning generally, context is one of the greatest assets here. This enables the reader to come to associate the same word correctly with different meanings, whether within the same language or across languages, e.g. to read Bank automatically as meaning a stool in the German textbook, and as referring to a bank in English; or to read fear automatically as meaning man in the Irish lesson and fear in the English lesson. Part of this process is one of overcoming interference from one language to the other, and sheer practice would seem to play a large part in this.

3. *Literal Understanding*

Prerequisite to literal understanding of matter read are correct word-recognition and association. At the primary level a considerable part of the teaching of reading amounted to teaching words which were already part of the pupil's vocabulary and experience. In so far as the learning-to-read process gives way to reading to learn, much of what is now read will be outside the pupil's range of experience or concepts. The secondary teacher therefore has both to teach new concepts, abstractions or ideas and at the same time the new words in which to crystallize these in the pupil's mind.

Some concepts and words are general enough to be encountered in several subjects, e.g. grammatical terms, and mathematical terms which enter into Geography or the physical sciences. On the other hand some of the difficulties in a subject as apparently non-technical as history may derive from that very fact. As Peel[14] points out, many recurring words in history such as church and law already 'carry existing personal and concrete meanings' which the pupil will tend to carry over erroneously to the reading task in history, thus leading to considerable misunderstandings. Of course, it is mainly through the technical vocabulary of each subject that learning occurs, and it is in this area therefore that the pupil must be taught to recognise and comprehend correctly each new term encountered, in the material to be read. There is a good deal of evidence available on the difficulties pupils have in coming to grips with the mere language of the history text and lesson,[15] not to mention other 'non-technical' subjects.

Literal understanding as such will be an important and perennial goal of language learning. The use of Cloze procedure[16] can be a valuable aid to the teacher in trying to gauge the readability of a particular book or essay for a given class, as well as an indication of their present levels of reading achievement in the language.

Halls[17] maintains that in the middle years of language learning the basic activity may well be reading – both towards achieving comprehension, learning vocabulary and grammar, and to develop conversational and pronunciation skills. Intensive reading, he holds consists of the teacher reading to pupils who are listening only, followed by the pupils seeing the text for the first time; the explanation of new vocabulary will either precede or follow these two steps. Extensive reading, on the other hand, while equally important, will move much faster, aiming at developing both reading fluency, general comprehension, and passive knowledge of new vocabulary or grammatical structures, rather than perfecting either pronunciation or other specifics. The choice of interesting material for extensive reading is important, as is the need to make this a more enjoyable experience for the class.

Mackey[18] also distinguishes between intensive and extensive reading, in language teaching, and besides stressing the importance of appropriately selected material for silent extensive reading, gives some useful criteria for its selection.

4. *Interpretation*

This is the process of inferring beyond the literal comprehension level, though the division between them may frequently be rather arbitrary. The reader now begins to read 'between the lines of the text', relating ideas together and referring them back to a familiar universe of discourse, or at least fitting them into a broader context than the text itself provides. If one accepts the dictum that there is no sentence that adequately states its own meaning, then at every level above that of mere word recognition, interpretation plays some role in reading. The judge interprets the law; the musician interprets the score, the mathematician interprets the formula. Interpretation is therefore 'the thinking side of comprehension'[16] involving the analysis of both the surface structure and the grammatical/syntactical or deep structure, all of which mediate between the concept and the language which conveys it.[17] In short, interpretation always entails 'going beyond the information given' to use Bartlett's phrase.[18]

A particular instance of this will be map-reading, where not only the symbols used but also what they tell us about the way of life, means of livelihood, and even cultural level of the inhabitants of a region must be read. But even requiring pupils to write written reports on a class visit to a factory, and subsequent comparison of different pupils' reports of the same visit, will itself illustrate to them the need to realise that we always do 'go beyond the information given', sometimes unwittingly or incorrectly and need to be made aware of this in interpreting written text.

5. *Evaluation*

The extent to which any reader can interpret text will depend, as with any thinking process, on his level of mental maturity. This applies particularly at the level of evaluative or critical reading. Questioning the text so as to distinguish fact from opinion or value judgement to determine the reliability of facts given, or the cogency of reasoning used, to evaluate the writer's real purpose or intention, all pre-suppose a capacity to think critically or independently in the first place. Self-confidence in dealing with this universe of discourse will be an important ingredient, as well as a growing awareness of the necessarily selective nature of any syllabus e.g. in history or geography, and therefore of the need to evaluate the art (or artifices) of any writer of a text or reference book. Spotting the anachronisms in out-of-date geography books, is itself becoming a necessary skill, as is the use of original documentary evidence in history. Whether we teach history to develop the pupil's understanding of human motives or his knowledge of historical events, or his appreciation of the historian's art, or some combination of all three, we must cultivate his power of critically reading primary as well as secondary sources.

But critical reading is scarcely a uniform skill of itself; it is more likely to occur when one is reading material within an area of specialised interest to oneself. Indeed the individual who reads critically in his own field may well be quite uncritical in reading outside it.

In a world saturated with print, most of it either bland or manipulative, the teacher must accept a responsiblity to cultivate in the pupil the habit of thinking and reading evaluatively. This cannot but mean developing a sceptical position towards the writer's intentions on occasion. But the same process also has its positive aspect in the cultivation of taste, of a sense of clarity, a feeling for style, etc. in the learner. Since in the final analysis education is a moral process, then it must be grounded in values and among these a love of truth, goodness and beauty must be central. Like every other medium, the printed word may either violate or uphold any or all of these, and the reader needs to be taught to evaluate written material for evidence that such values are either being vindicated or violated. In history, for instance, a lesson on the Armada might juxtapose textbooks written for English schools with those written for Spanish schools, to illustrate the need to apply criteria of truth even to the school texts being used.

Conclusion

Reading is something no one can really do for you. In view of the current shift in the teacher's role from that of dispenser of facts or knowledge to that of facilitator of new learning, the pupil's need to become an independent reader in each area of the curriculum, as the key in *learning to learn*, can scarcely be exaggerated.

It is misleading to assume that reading is a single skill which, once mastered, will be applied by the pupil in learning any area of the secondary school curriculum. On the contrary, explicitly cultivating the pupil's skill in reading textbooks, reference material, etc. in any given subject, is proposed as intrinsic to the teaching of each subject. While this developmental teaching of reading will not take the same form as the teaching of basic reading skills in the primary school, nevertheless it will be based upon and dovetail with what has gone before.

It is difficult to imagine reading in the school context that does not result in some assimilation of new information, new ideas, new purposes. Piaget based the cognitive development of the individual on the twin processes of assimilation and accommodation – assimilation of the new, and accommodation of existing mental structures to this. At the secondary school stage, the pupil's growing capacity for 'formal', logical thinking begins to release his thinking from the limitations of the concrete, the particular and the immediate in time and place; to think logically and in a more universalistic manner. He also moves from more descriptive to more explanatory thinking[14] and learns to set targets or goals for his own learning tasks rather than rely on others to do this for him.

This whole process facilitates the growth of reading ability, and is in turn enhanced by it. The mind grows by what it feeds on, and so does literacy. The fact that the latter is now seen as an increasingly powerful tool of learning should not obscure the need to sharpen the tool itself.

The secondary stage is also a crucial one for the crystallization of reading habits, tastes and interests, or alternatively for their decline. Lifelong strategies, styles, attitudes and personal commitment to reading may depend directly therefore on the pre-emptive influence of what is achieved or overlooked by the secondary school teacher.

References and Bibliography

1. DeBoer, J. and Whipple G. "Reading development in other curriculum Areas", in Witty, Paul A. *Development in and through Reading*, 60th Yearbook of the NSSE, Part 1, Chicago: Univ. of Chicago, 1961. Cited in Downing J. *Comparative Reading: cross-national studies of behaviour and processes in Reading and Writing.* New York, The Macmillan Company, 1973, pp. 508-9.
2. Ramsey, W.Z. (1963) "The Kentucky Reading Study". *The Reading Teacher* 16, 178-181.
3. Artley, A.S. (1968) *Trends and Practices in Secondary Reading*, Newark, Delaware, International Reading Association.
4. Dearborn and Rothney (1941) *Predicting the Child's Development.* Cambridge, Mass. Sci-Art. p. 306.
5. Lenneberg, E.H. (1967) *Biological Foundations of Language.* New York, Wiley.
6. Wall, W.D. (1960) *Adolescents in School and Society*, Slough National Foundation for Educational Research.
7. Schonell, F.J. (1942) *Backwardness in the Basic Subjects*, Edinburgh, Oliver and Boyd.
8. Young, C. "A Qualitative Analysis of Reading Achievement in Edmonton Schools". *Alberta Journal of Educational Research*, 1956, 2, 135-150.
9. Sheldon, M.D. "The Nature and Scope of Reading Programmes adapted to to-day's Needs: in the Upper Grades and the Junior High School" In *Better Readers for Our Times*, International Reading Association Conference Proceedings, New York: Scholastic Magazines, 30-33.
10. Foster, G.L. "Freshman Problems: 44% couldn't read their tests." In *The Clearing House*, 1955, 29, 414-417.
11. Swan, T.D. *Reading Standards in Irish Schools*, Dublin, The Educational Company, 1978.
12. Swan, T.D. "A Diagnostic Approach to Teaching Reading to Young Adolescents". In P. Widlake (Ed.) *Remedial Education, Programmes and Progress.* London, Longman for the National Association for Remedial Education, pp. 184-192, 1977.
13. Smith, Frank: *Understanding Reading: a psycholinguistic analysis of reading and learning to read.* New York, Holt Rinehart and Winston, 1978.
14. Peel, E.A.: *The Pupil's Thinking*. London, Oldbourne, 1960.
15. Steel, Ian: *Developments in History Teaching*, London, Open Books, 1976.
16. O'Callaghan, M.F.: Aural and Oral Examinations – from theory to practice. M.A. Thesis, Education Department, U.C.D. 1980.
17. Halls, W.D.: 'The Teaching of Languges'. In A.D.C. Peterson (Ed.) *Techniques of Teaching*, Volume 2, Secondary Education. Oxford, Pergamon, 1966.
18. Mackey, W.F.: *Language Teaching Analysis.* London, Longmans,

1965, pp. 279-281.

19. Tinker, M.A. and McCullough, C.: *Teaching Elementary Reading* (3rd Ed) Appleton-Century-Crofts. Cited in T.L. Harris and R.E. Hodges (Eds.) *A Dictionary of Reading and Related Terms.* Delaware, International Reading Association, 1981.
20. Schwartz, D., Sparkman, J. and Deese, J. Cited in T.L. Harris and R.E. Hodges (Eds) *A Dictionary of Reading and Related Terms,* Delaware, International Reading Association, 1981.
21. Bartlett, F.C. *Thinking.* Manchester Memoirs, 93, 3 (The Clayton Memorial Lecture).

2. *Developing Reading Skills in the Post-infant Years*

Jessie Reid, University of Edinburgh

It has been increasingly recognised, over the last decade, that it was wrong to think of the teaching of reading as a task to be completed by the infant teachers in the primary school and that these infant teachers ideally pass on to the Junior stage children who (in quotes) "can read."

One of the first people to produce extensive evidence on this sensitive area in primary education, and to speak out boldly on the needs of children in the lower Junior years, was Dr. Joyce Morris. In her book *Standards and Progress in Reading*[1] she made the following comment on her findings in the schools of Kent:

> Findings of the survey indicated that the reading standards of seven-year-olds were such that nearly half of them still needed the kind of teaching associated with the infant school.

The figures which backed up this assertion showed that 19 per cent of children aged seven were still at – or below – the level of a first primer, and a further 26 per cent were not beyond the third book in the scheme they were using. Morris points out elsewhere in her book that the standards in Kent were not untypical of standards in England and Wales as a whole, and that the inescapable conclusion was therefore that teachers at the Junior stage needed to know how to teach reading at many levels, being prepared when necessary to deal with children's quite elementary problems in finding out what the print "says."

Morris's survey also revealed, however, that 75 per cent of the teachers of first-year Juniors had not received any training in infant methods, 52 per cent had no experience of infant teaching, and 18 per cent had neither training nor experience in infant work. Most teachers of lower Juniors, therefore, were ill-equipped by training and experience for one of the crucial tasks facing them.

The statistics on which this 1966 book was based were already almost ten years old when they were published, and are now twenty years old; and in the intervening time things have begun to change. Most notably, over the whole of Great Britain, there have been changes in the area of teacher training, including the institution of numerous diploma courses in the teaching of reading.

Interesting recent information comes from a survey of conditions in training institutions in England and Wales conducted by Cook and Moyle.[2] They found that the average figure for lecture hours devoted to reading, for teachers training at Junior level, was around 40 in Colleges of Education, around 50 in Colleges of Higher Education, and ranging from 10 to 89 in other institutions. The authors point out, however, that these figures come "nowhere near the target figure of 150 hours for language and reading courses suggested by the Bullock Committee."

The Report of the Bullock Committee[3] especially when taken together with the earlier Report of the James Committee[4] on teacher training, has contributed to giving to the teaching of reading throughout the primary school an explicit importance which it has never quite achieved in the past. But when we compare what is being proposed in these reports which the observations made in 1966 by Morris, we find that there has been a distinct change of emphasis. Much of the discussion is now concerned not with continuing the basic instruction characteristic of the infant department, but with "extending study skills," "training in the use of dictionaries," "learning to read in the content areas," "appreciation and evaluation" – in other words, with applications of reading, and kinds of reading, that are often called "higher" as opposed to "basic", and which have as their uniting characteristic an emphasis on meaning, purpose and relevance.

No one who wishes to see children ultimately enjoying reading as a cultural activity and using it effectively as a vehicle of education would quarrel with such a list of aims as I have indicated. But notice that it goes back to pre-supposing the very thing which Joyce Morris was at pains to show did not hold for about 50 per cent of 7-year-old children – namely a basic competence in what one might call "processing" the printed word. For instance, all activities involving searching for specific words or specific pieces of information – activities involving dictionaries, or single books of reference, pre-suppose the ability to recognise what you are looking for when you see it. There is no point in asking a child to look in a reference book for the mention of, say, "migration," or "nocturnal animals," or "Stonehenge," unless he can read these words so easily that they jump out of the page to meet his eye. So that is my first point. An enthusiasm for initiating children into the *uses* of literacy, (which will of course eventually make literacy meaningful to them) must not blind us to those limitations which will prevent all but the better readers from being able to take these leaps into a new domain.

But there is more to be said. Much of my own thinking and research has been concerned with the kinds of understanding and learning that have to accompany and support the learning of literacy; and I have been for some years greatly concerned with the nature of the transition from being a child in the input department, working through a basic scheme, to being a child in the middle Juniors, reading silently, reading anthologies which contain a variety of styles, and reading simple textbooks and books of reference in order to learn from them.

Many children simply do not make this transition; and although some fail because they are still struggling with elementary "processing," others fail for different reasons, and it is to these reasons that I want now to turn.

Let me take first the matter of learning to read silently. At the annual Conference of UKRA,[5] I spoke on the topic of "Becoming a Reader", and I want to quote again something which I quote there. It is not from an official document – it is from the writing of a gifted and perspicacious man of letters who remembered his childhood with vividness and was moved to reflect on the acquisition of the skill of silent reading.

His name was Robert Louis Stevenson. Here is what he wrote:

> To pass from hearing literature to reading it is to take a great and dangerous step. With not a few, I think a large proportion of their pleasure then comes to an end . . . they read thenceforward by the eye alone and hear never again the chime of fair words or the march of the stately period . . . But to all the step is dangerous, it involves coming of age; it is even a kind of second weaning. In the past, all was at the choice of others . . . In future we are to approach the silent inexpressive type alone, like pioneers . . .

This passage is remarkable on many counts, not least of these being its date: it was written in 1879. But I want to select two points from it. Stevenson is concerned with the reading of literature – of writing which has some intrinsic and abiding merit of content and style – and with that component of the language which is appreciated *through the ear*. Earlier in the essay from which this extract is taken Stevenson laid great emphasis on the vital role played by the stories and rhymes read and recited to him by his nurse – an emphasis now endorsed by much contemporary research and thinking.[6] And Stevenson's own prose is outstandingly rhythmic and melodious. What he is obviously implying in the passage I quoted is that our sense of the "chime of fair words" should not necessarily disappear when the skill of silent reading is developed, and that reading "by the eye alone" can be a loss and not a gain.

Nowadays, children normally make, of course, two transitions – to reading silently from being read to by someone else, and to reading silently from reading aloud themselves. I should like to endorse very strongly the suggestion made in the Bullock Report that these three activities should be linked and intermingled much more than they often are; but I should like to suggest further that the intermingling should extend well into the Junior stages – perhaps right through into secondary school. Of course, not everything which children read calls for enhancement by being heard, but allowing them to listen to the reading aloud of poetry or good prose *as part of their reading lesson* will help them to cultivate that inner ear which can add so much to the enjoyment of a well-written narrative.

The second point in Stevenson's comment concerns the change from the shared, communal activity of being read to (or of reading aloud to an adult) to the solitary exploration of a book in silence. The children now have to "approach the silent, inexpressive type alone . . . like pioneers." Not only is the book silent – it is, as it were, devoid of signposts. There is very little to tell the child what to expect, and – if a book is of his own choosing – whether he has chosen wisely. Many teachers argue for letting children choose their own books for free reading time. But we all know from our experience how mistaken even we can be in a book chosen from a library shelf or picked up in a bookshop. We need to exercise care, then, over the stage at which we let children make their choices unaided and read without some guidance. Many a child has been turned away from reading at a crucial stage by finding that what looked like an inviting path turns into a thicket of thorns.

I want now to move to the second aspect of the three-fold transition which I am considering, namely the learning to read a variety of styles and registers. During the last ten years, and largely as a result of those studies which have looked at early reading as a language-learning activity, opinion has been moving towards the view that the material on which children first "cut their teeth" in reading should be modelled on the sentence structures which they have mastered in their speech and which they commonly produce. By "sentence structures common in speech" we are not to understand colloquialisms, nor yet long passages of dialogue. Rather, the phrase implies the use of characteristic sequences, or patterns, in the *syntax* of children's speech, built into simple narrative and descriptive prose. At the same time the phrase implies that forms which belong to the language of books or to the language of oral story telling should be excluded. These ideas are discussed at length in 'The Written Word', which is the Teacher's Manual for *Link-Up*.[7]

Children must, however, come sooner or later to reading prose which makes use of some of the infinite resources of stylistic variation of which our written language is capable. Many instances of these are so familiar to us that we hardly notice them, even though many of them are things we only read or write, and would never say. For instance, no one ever *says*: "Suddenly, baring his teeth in a menacing growl, the hair bristling on his back, there appeared a huge black dog." But such a sentence is fairly standard in the telling of a story with drama and tension. What we would say might be more like this: "Suddenly a huge black dog appeared. He was growling and baring his teeth and the hair on his back was bristling."

The words in the second version are much the same as in the first: the difference is in the *syntax*. And the view we now have of the reading process makes it abundantly clear that *syntax makes for difficulty on its own*, apart from vocabulary. One of the major learning tasks for children in the early Junior years is the acquisition of an increasing store of syntactic knowledge, so that they recognise sentence patterns in a way similar to that in which they recognise words. If they do not do this, what they read will not make sense, and comprehension will fail.

The language of non-fiction, of which children in the Junior years have to read so much, has to be mastered gradually in the same way. I have already drawn attention to the emphasis now being put, in statements of policy such as the Bullock Report, on reading activities which involve searching for information, distinguishing detail from main ideas, having a specific and conscious purpose in mind, or formulating a question and looking for the answer to it in a piece of text. Most of these activities belong in the context of "reading for information" or "reading to learn." They therefore pre-suppose some degree of ability to make sense of the texts in question. But the syntax and phraseology of non-fiction have characteristics all their own, different from those found in story-telling, and it follows from a language-based view of reading that these characteristics must become familiar before comprehension is possible. So the teaching of reading has to include helping children to extend their syntactic grasp of phraseology like:

> Long as it is, a giraffe's neck will not bend.
> There are many foxes in Britain, but *it requires both care and luck to see them.*
> *Not everyone lives in a town or city.*

(All these are actual examples from information books for 7 to

8 year-olds.) Apart from the word "requires," the *words* in all three sentences are very easy. But in each one, the *syntax* is unlike that of everyday speech, and characteristic of the register of informational writing. In each case, the meaning needs discussion even if children can recognise the words.

Once children are able to follow the meaning of text with some of these features, they can of course be given tasks which represent the beginnings of "study." They can be encouraged to go back to something they have read and look again, perhaps more thoughtfully than at first. They can be asked why one word rather than another is used, what can be inferred though it is not stated, how one piece of information is linked with another. This kind of reflection on the text, if it does not become a tedious drill (which it must not do) will in turn enhance their reading by heightening their awareness of the language, and should help their written work. But I would in passing plead for some fresh thought on the respective importance of being able to read and being able to write. If we leave aside school exercises and examinations, the average citizen does not need to be able to *write* at a literary level, though he needs to be functionally literate and to be able to spell. But he *does* need – desperately – to be able to read and to speak articulately. I want to suggest a re-adjustment of emphasis in language work, to give more time to reading and talking, and less to 'creative' writing until reading ability and oral communication are well established.

The task of the teacher of children aged 7 to 11 in the area of reading, seems then to have four main aspects. It calls, as Joyce Morris pointed out and as we know from experience, for a continuation of basic help in word-recognition, in phonics, and in acquiring fluency with simple straightforward text. It calls for the skilled weaning of children from dependence on a shared activity and on reading aloud to the enjoyment of reading simple fiction and non-fiction silently on their own. It calls for the ability to extend the children's linguistic resources so that these encompass more of the variety of language used by different writers of stories; and it calls for a similar carefully graded introduction of the kinds of reading that we usually call "study," accompanied by appropriate language extension involving syntax just as much as vocabulary.

If these are the tasks, then the teacher needs material with which to carry them out. There is a special need for reading material to bridge the dangerous gulf between basic schemes and books for the self-reliant reader. What frequently happens duing this vital period of development is that the material on which children work with their teachers, or which they are invited to read closely, consists of relatively short stories, or brief pieces of description or narrative lifted from a larger whole. While these can have a place in the child's reading experience, they are no substitute for more extended and complete writing which allows for the development of a plot, the revelation of character, or the pursuit of a theme. Too often, children meet extended writing only when left to themselves; yet many of them need to be helped to sustain interest and to follow the unfolding of a tale. A reading diet of nothing but snippets will leave this gap unfilled, and Stevenson's remarks on the need for children to become "pioneers" spring once again to mind. A pioneer needs to know how to find his way, and to be self-sustaining. Professional writers for children, whether in the field of fiction or of school subjects, need to realise that good writing can be – and ought to be – straightforward, and that many of the difficulties children exhibit in reading are produced not by incapacity but by the needlessly complex nature of the writing.

I believe that if we could successfully bring about a widened vision of the teaching of reading right through Primary school, and an awakening to the realities on the part of authors – a realisation of what ordinary children can read and understand – we might see a more literate, and more self-respecting population of children entering our secondary schools.

Robert Louis Stevenson called children's literature "a delightful dress-rehearsal of experience." It should be our aim to bring all our children into the audience.

References and Bibliography

1. Morris, J.M. *Standards and Progress in Reading.* Slough: National Foundation for Educational Research, 1966.
2. Cook, H. and Moyle, D. The state of Reading Teacher Training. *Reading Education*, No. 2., March 1977, pp. 36-47.
3. Department of Education and Science. *A Language for Life.* (The

Bullock Report) London: HMSO, 1975.
4. Department of Education and Science. *Teacher Education and Training.* (The James Report) London: HMSO, 1972.
5. Reid, J.F. *Becoming a Reader.* Paper read at the Annual Conference of United Kingdom Reading Association, 1977.
6. Clarke, M.M. *Young Fluent Readers.* London: Heinemann Educational Books, 1976.
7. Reid, J. and Low, J. *The Written Word.* (Revised Edition). Edinburgh: Holmes McDougall, 1977.
8. Stevenson, R.L. *Essays of Travel.* London: Chatto & Windus, 1924.

3. *A Remedial Programme Based on a Diagnostic Test for Irish Pupils*

Michael Lynch, Education Department, University College, Dublin

Introduction

In 1976 primary schools in a provincial Irish centre cooperated with the writer in testing pupils in standards V and VI with a view to developing a diagnostic reading test which would be closely related to the content of instruction. Thirty teachers in thirteen schools participated and just over one thousand students were tested – the total school population in the local schools at this level. Written responses were obtained for all students on seven hundred items covering many aspects of vocabulary. The response matrix of almost three-quarters of a million entries was extensively analysed by means of Rasch-Wright procedures.

The purpose of this paper is *not* to report on the construction of the diagnostic test but to discuss a remedial programme with twenty students in one of the sample schools who were identified as having severe reading problems. The remedial programme began in December 1976 and continued until June 1977 with the assistance of the Irish Department of Education. Pupils were withdrawn from their normal class for one and a half hours, three mornings per week, in groups of ten. They also received individual instruction at other times during the day, apart from normal class instruction. Every effort was made to utilise the test information diagnostically in planning the remedial programme.

This paper discusses problems inherent in this approach in general terms and illustrates ways in which information from the test was used to plan instruction by reference to a student's response.

Diagnostic Tests as a Basis of Remediation

Global cognitive measures such as the Stanford-Binet and the Wechsler Intelligence Scale for Children provide very limited information with which to guide subsequent instructional programmes. Yet clearly there is a demand, particularly from the field of special education, for diagnostic profiles which will reveal intraindividual differences and indicate areas in need of remediation.[1] Unfortunately, instruments constructed with this end continually in mind have had only mixed success. The Illinois Test of Psycholinguistic Abilities[2] seeks to analyse the child's psycholinguistic abilities along three dimensions deemed to be important; these are (a) channels of communication (auditory-vocal; visual-motor), (b) processes (receptions; organisation; expression), and (c) levels of organisation or complexity (automatic level: representational level). The classification of specific functions should give clues to possible remedial action.[3] In her study of young fluent readers Clark[4] observed that the results of the ITPA added little of diagnostic value for the fluent readers when taken in association with their scores which were already known from other language tests, and when compared with profiles of children known to have reading difficulties. She urges caution in planning remedial programmes based on deficits shown on such tests. A comparison of the results for the fluent readers and of the backward readers of average intelligence of nine years was striking not for the differences in the profiles but for their similarity!

The Frostig Developmental Test of Visual Perception claims to measure five relatively unrelated but important areas of visual perception.[5] The test has been vigorously attacked and the claims that identification of strengths and weaknesses followed by appropriate training exercises resulted in improved scores have been greeted with scepticism.[6] Tew has stated that over ten years it has come to be regarded uncritically as an efficient diagnostic instrument for the identification of perceptual handicaps which are presumed to contribute to difficulties in acquiring skills.[7] Tew's own study in South Wales is cited as an example of research which does not substantiate the Frostig claims.

Olson[8] and Smith and Marx[9] in the United States found no relationship between Frostig subtest scores or the perceptual quotient and the reading ability of normal school children. Tew cites the Scandinavian study of Neilsen and Ringe[10] where it was observed that the Frostig test did not discriminate between retarded and normal readers. In fairness it must be stated that subsequent issues of Remedial Education carried correspondence critical of Tew.[11]

Profiles

Since profiling was central to the diagnostic programme under consideration, some observations on the concept would seem apposite. The notion of profiling across different aspects of reading performance carries enormous intuitive appeal. Zig-zag lines linking high and low points on a graph do produce a most striking graphical display. Doe in a recent article in the Times Educational Supplement[12] reproduced one such appealing profile for the Richmond Tests of Basic skills.[13] This test has been adopted by Cumbria and a special grid for Richmond test scores included in the county's new record card.

One hopes that the teachers will treat such profiling with professional caution. The special problems relating to differential diagnosis have always been clear to test constructors but unfortunately in popular treatment they have been either ignored or glossed over. In the zig-zag treatment the standard error attached to the different scores tends to be ignored. Bookbinder[14] says "most teachers are about as interested in the standard error of a test as most politicians are in the standard error of a vote-predicting public opinion poll (p. 21)."

A more sophisticated version of the zig-zag treatment regards attainment on a subtest not as a fixed point but as a band varying within one or two standard errors of a midpoint. This enables statements to be made with precisely stated statistical confidence about an individual's score. According to this scheme a profile across subtests will appear as a series of vertical bands arranged across the page. Where the bands overlap little significance can be attached to score differences.

Visual discrepancies between high and low points do not necessarily indicate obvious areas of weakness. One has to consider the intercorrelations between the subtests as well as subtest reliabilities.[15] Unfortunately unwarranted interpretations are far too common; Savage[16] says "interpreting subtest scores without regard for statistical considerations is a common practice which should be strongly discouraged, if not banned (p. 35)." Even greater difficulties arise when different norm groups are utilized in the construction of the subtests and when profiling is then attempted across the composite tests. The APA Standards[16a] urge great caution with such mixed scales. Reputable tests will warn of the dangers and the mistakes of attaching too much weight to every discrepancy in scores, e.g. the manuals of the Edinburgh Reading Tests. Less acceptable tests may not even report the intercorrelations and separate subtests' reliabilities and seek to ignore the problem! AERA's Technical Recommendations state that "if the manual recommends that diagnostic interpretations be based on the test profile, evidence should be provided that the profile patterns used are valid discriminators."[17]

Reporting in terms of spelling or reading ages is even more suspect,[18] despite their popularity with teachers. The objections are fully discussed in Vincent and Cresswell[19]. Obviously the preferred units of teachers do not coincide with those of the research workers![14] Problems in score interpretation are not confined to measure of attainment. In the field of guidance and counselling some interest questionnaires provide ipsative scores, i.e. multiple scores summing to a constant. These scores are open to even greater misinterpretation.[20]

Rasch Scales

Test items were extensively analysed and calibrated by Rasch-Wright procedures. A value was assigned to each of the 700 items – its "difficulty" on an interval scale extending from -6 to +6. The Rasch model is probabilistic in nature and lies within the context of latent trait theories of which it is a special case. In latent trait terminology person attainment is described as person "ability." When person ability is exactly the same as item difficulty the person has got a 50/50 chance of correctly answering an item. Both item difficulty and person ability values are on the same interval scale. The chances of success can be precisely stated.

From person performance on a given cluster of items, a subtest, it is possible to estimate person ability values corresponding to different score groups, just as one can convert raw scores to standard scores in a conventional test manual. In the case of Rasch analysis the ability values are not standard scores or grade norms but values which lie along the same interval scale as the item difficulties. A good introduction to this method of scaling is provided in the report to the Schools' Council by Willmott and Fowles;[21] Baker[22] also provides a recent account within the context of advances in item analysis. The method has been applied to test construction in the U.S.A. in the Woodcock Reading Mastery Test.[23] Rasch would claim that the result of this kind of item calibration is a measure of person ability which is independent of the items attempted. This claim has important consequences for instructional programmes. Items presented to a person after the treatment period need not be the same as before, they can even be at a higher level of difficulty. It is only necessary that they fit the Rasch model. This claim was stringently tested in the preparation of the main dissertation and certainly was quite convincing for the data.

Application

Consideration of an individual student may serve to relate the foregoing discussion to the remedial programme. One student was 13 years at the beginning of the remedial programme. His profile was based on his results in the district-wide testing programme when he was in sixth standard. At the end of that year he was independently assessed by the local Vocational school and was considered too low in reading attainment to benefit from the courses. He repeated sixth standard in the primary school and it was during that year that he took part in the remedial classes. His ability (attainment) on a subtest of Homophones was -0.06 on the scale. The average Rasch value for this subtest was +0.81 for V standard (*N* = 494), and +1.39 for VI standard (*N* = 520). His value was thus well below the mean for sixth class. Let us consider in some depth the meaning of the score of -0.06. In the Homophones subtest the student was asked to write "a word which sounded exactly the same as the given word, but had a different meaning and spelling." Sufficient examples were provided, e.g. flea, flee; cent, sent; hymn, him. The subtest had two parallel forms with a subtest reliability of +0.92. Combined raw scores on the two parallel forms correlated +0.79 (*N* = 541) with combined raw scores on the Vocabulary and Spelling subtests of the Drumcondra English Test, Level III. At the level of individual items the student's ability value of -0.06 would give him a probability of 0.50 of responding to the following items.

Item	*Correct Response*	*Item Difficulty*	*Student's Response*
1. nun	none	-0.027	incorrect
2. scene	seen	-0.133	correct
3. chord	cord	-0.113	correct
4. haul	hall	-0.092	correct
5. prey	pray	-0.092	correct
6. cruise	crews	+3.019	incorrect

For the first four the student had a probability of about 0.5 for no. 5 about 0.90 and for no. 6 "cruise" only about 0.05 because of the item's difficulty.

In the subtest Prefixes the student was required to encircle the prefixes for 27 items after sufficient examples and explanation. The student's Rasch value on this subtest was +0.60 Bear this in mind in considering the items below:

Item	*Prefix*	*Difficulty*	*Student's Response*
1. overgrown	over-	-2.723	correct
2. enmesh	en-	-1.584	correct

3. cooperate	co-	+.0711	incorrect
4. circumnavigate	circum-	+0.814	incorrect
5. perinatal	peri-	+1.556	incorrect
6. contradictory	contra-	+2.606	correct
7. infrastructure	infra-	+2.176	incorrect

At the beginning of the programme the student showed the following deficits on well-known tests:

Neale Analysis of Reading Ability:	minus 5 yrs. 5 mths.
Schonell Spelling Form A	minus 5 yrs.
Marino	minus 4 yrs. 9 mths.

Similar analyses were made for all students in the remedial class and the information incorporated in the remedial programme. Their scores and responses were available at all times to the students and they were encouraged to examine their responses and to relate them to the item difficulties.

Analysis of performance took into account responses to individual items rather than summed scores. Clinical observations were made on persistence and individual styles of response as has been advocated by Eysenck.[24] The students' involvement provided a sense of purpose and contributed to the success of the remedial programme. Vygotsky[25] believed that the child has little sense of purpose in writing and has only a vague idea of its usefulness. By focusing on individual items it was possible to overcome this. Students began to look at words with curiosity and interest, a necessary prerequisite for success, as was eloquently described by Peters.[26] It did much to dispel the state of confusion with which many readers enter the task. Every effort was made to prevent the work degenerating into a series of arid and meaningless exercises and to remove the drudgery of what could have become meaningless drill.

Obviously no one source of material can be regarded as comprehensive and adequate. The List referred to by Peters[27] was found to be particularly useful.[28] The pupils spent most of their day in the normal classroom and the contribution of the class teacher is not to be underrated. It is felt that the continuous contribution of diagnosis to teaching helped.[29]

References and Bibliography

1. Ward, J. On the concept of criterion-referenced measurement. *British Journal of Educational Psychology*, 1970, *40*, 314-323.
2. Kirk, S.A., McCarthy, J., and Kirk, W. *Illinois test of psycholinguistic abilities.* (Rev. ed.) Urbana, Ill.: University of Illinois Press, 1968.
3. Paraskevopoulos, J.N., & Kirk, S.A. *The developmental and psychometric characteristics of the revised Illinois test of psycholinguistic abilities.* Urbana, Ill.: University of Illinois Press, 1969.
4. Clark, M.M. *Young fluent readers.* London: Heinemann Educational, 1976.
5. Frostig, M. *Frostig developmental test of visual perception.* Consulting Psychologists Press, 1963.
6. Pumfrey, P.D. *Reading: tests and assessment techniques.* London: Hodder and Stoughton, 1976.
7. Tew, B. Some doubts about the Frostig test of visual perception. *Remedial Education,* 1976, *11*(1), 32-5.
8. Olson, A.V. Factor analytic studies of the Frostig developmental test of visual perception. Journal of Special Education, 1968, *2*, 429.
9. Smith, P.A. and Marx, R.W. Some cautions on the use of the Frostig test. *Journal of Learning Disabilities*, 1972, *6*, 357.
10. Neilsen, H.H., and Ringe, K. Visuo-perceptive and visuo-motor performance of children with reading disabilities. *Scandinavian Journal of Psychology,* 1969, 10, 225. cited by Tew (1976).
11. Topping, K.J. Correspondence. *Remedial Education*, 1976, *11*(2), 89.
12. Doe, B. Testing time for kids. *Times Educational Supplement* 19.8.'77.
13. Hieronymus, A., Lindquist, E., & France, N. *Richmond test of basic skills.* London: Nelson, 1974, 1975.
14. Bookbinder, G.E. Reading ages and standardized scores. *Reading,* 1976, *10*, 3, 20-3.
15. Anastasi, A. *Psychological testing.* (3rd ed.) New York: Macmillan, 1968.
16. Savage, R.D. *Psychometric assessment of the individual child.* Harmondsworth: Penguin Books, 1968.

16a. American Psychological Association, *Standards for educational and psychological tests and manuals.* Washington D.C.: American Psychological Association, Inc., 1966.

17. AERA, *Technical recommendations for achievement tests.* Washington D.C.: National Education Association, 1955. p. 25, c.11.
18. Vincent, D. Reading ages and NFER reading tests. *Educational Research*, 1974, *16*(3), 1976-80.
19. Vincent, D. and Cresswell, M. *Reading tests in the classroom.* Windsor, Berks.' National Foundation for Educational Research Publishing Company, 1976.
20. Closs, S.J. Ipsative vs. normative interpretations of interest test scores. *Bulletin of the British Psychological Society*, 1976, *29*, 289-99.
21. Willmott, A.S., and Fowles, D. *The objective interpretation of school*

performance. Windsor, Berks.: National Foundation for Educational Research Publishing Company, 1974.

22. Baker, F.B. Advances in item analysis. *Review of Educational Research*, 1977, *47*(1), 151-78.
23. Woodcock, R.W. *Woodcock reading mastery tests.* Circle Pines, Minnesota: American Guidance Services Ltd., 1973.
24. Eysenck, H.J. Intelligence assessment: a theoretical and experimental approach. *British Journal of Educational Psychology,* 1967, *37,* 81-98.
25. Vygotsky, L.S. *Thought and language.* Cambridge, Mass.: M.I.T. Press, 1962.
26. Peters, M.L. *Diagnostic and remedial spelling manual.* London: Macmillan, 1975.
27. Peters, M.L. *Success in spelling.* Cambridge: Institute of Education, 1970.
28. New Zealand Council for Educational Research Alphabetical Spelling List. Exeter: Wheaton, 1963.
29. Farr, R. *Reading: What can be measured?* Newark, Delaware: International Reading Association, 1968.
30. Godfrey Thomson Unit, University of Edinburgh, *Edinburgh Reading Tests*, Stage 2. London: Hodder & Stoughton, 1972.
31. Lynch, Michael: The Construction of Diagnostic Reading Scales for Senior Primary and Lower post-primary students in Irish schools by means of Rasch Item Analysis. Unpublished Doctoral dissertation, Education Department, University College, Dublin, 1978.
32. Moray House College of Education, *Edinburgh reading tests*, Stage 3, London: Hodder and Stoughton, 1972.
33. Pumfrey, P.D. Reading measurement and evaluation: some current concerns and promising developments. In J. Gilliland (Ed.), *Reading: research and classroom practice.* London: Ward Lock Educational for United Kingdom Reading Association, 1977.

4. *The Fernald Technique in Remedial Reading*

Ellen O'Leary, Education Department, University College, Dublin

Most teachers who have been engaged in the remediation of reading difficulties, will have come across the very severely disabled reader – the non-reader. This child is characterised by his failure to make progress, despite considerable help, encouragement and effort. Even when there is no primary emotional problem inhibiting learning, when visual and auditory perception seem adequate and motivation is normal, such a child fails to respond to the more usual remedial procedures. He acquires only a tentative grasp of a very limited vocabulary and may fail to identify these words consistently over time.

It is generally accepted that initially, when a child learns to read he does so by converting or translating the visual word into its auditory equivalent. A small minority of children however appear to lack transmodal facilitation and for them substantial and intractable problems arise in learning to read. For such children the Fernald technique offers hope.

The Fernald Technique

In the 1930s Dr. Grace Fernald and her co-workers developed a technique for helping children with this severe type of reading difficulty. In 1943 the first comprehensive account of the Fernald technique was published.[1]

This technique is a VAKT (Visual, auditory, kinesthetic, tactile) method whereby the child finger-traces the word while articulating it. Thus there is an integration of the visual, auditory, kinesthetic and tactile sensory inputs, each reinforcing the other. The child hears, sees and says the word and feels it with both his proprioceptive and tactile receptors. Consequently, where there is some weakness in the transmodal facilitation between the auditory and the visual systems, this multisensory stimulation helps to establish or strengthen the neural interconnections necessary for this kind of learning.

The stages of the Fernald technique

There are four identifiable stages in this technique which, to be really effective, must be used within a language experience approach to reading.

Stage 1. The child is invited to try a new way of learning words. He is allowed to select any word he wishes to learn, regardless of length and this word is taught to him, in the following manner:

> The chosen word is written for the child, with crayon on cardboard, in plain, blackboard-size, cursive writing or print. The child traces the word with finger contact, saying the word aloud as he traces it. The teacher is careful to note that he does not merely spell out the word. The child is helped to develop gradually the facility to co-ordinate the saying of the word with the tracing of it, and care is taken that the pronunciation is natural and not stilted.

The child repeats this process as many times as is necessary, until he can write the word correctly without referring to the copy. When he has written the word correctly from memory, at least twice, he now uses it in his story. When the story has been written by the child, following the above procedures with needed words, he files the newly learned words under the appropriate letters in his word file. His story is subsequently typed for him and he reads it in print.

Stage 2. This is the stage when it is no longer necessary for the child to finger-trace the word. The word is written by the teacher as in Stage 1. After a certain period of tracing, the child develops the ability to learn any new word (but not new in his oral vocabulary) by simply looking at the word in script, saying it over to himself, as he looks at it, and then writing it from memory articulating it as he writes. It is as if he now internalises the previously overt action of tracing.

The child continues to write freely and to read the printed copy of what he has written. Writing is by this time so well established that the child's stories are usually much longer and more complicated than they were at first.

Explanatory Notes on Stages I and II

1. Finger contact is important in tracing. The word is always traced with the finger in contact with the paper. Fernald found that the learning rate is much more rapid with finger contact than when pencil or pen is used.
2. At no point does the child copy words. Looking back and forth from the word he is writing to the copy, causes the child to break the word up into small and sometimes meaningless units. The flow of the hand in writing the word is also interrupted and the eye movements consist of a shifting back and forth from the word to the copy, instead of eye movements adjusting to the word as it is being written. Indeed the writing of the word without the copy is important at all stages of learning to read and spell. This theory is supported by Peters[2] in her work on the teaching of spelling. Fernald herself condemned the copying of words as a most serious block to learning to write them correctly and to recognising them after they have been written.
3. The word being learned is always written as a unit. In case of error or interruption in writing the word, the incorrect form is covered or completely erased. The child then starts the word again and writes it as a whole. Not infrequently it may be necessary for him to refer to the copy or to trace it again before he can write it correctly. The word is never patched up by merely erasing the incorrect part and substituting the correction.
4. The child says each part of the word either to himself or aloud as he writes it, for it is important to establish the association between the sound of the word and its form, so

that eventually the visual stimulus alone will be sufficient to evoke the correct response.

5. It is important too, that this vocalisation of the word should be natural – that it should be a repetition of the word as it actually sounds and not a stilted, distorted sounding out of letters or syllables in such a way that the word is lost in the process. It takes a little practice to synchronise the articulation of the word with the hand and arm movement involved in tracing and writing it, but after a brief period, this is usually achieved.
6. Words are always used in context. The essential thing is that the child should be using his own oral language resources and mastering the task of communicating his ideas through the use of the written word. However, to record even one sentence may require that he learn a number of words. Consequently, he is not encouraged to write long complex sentences initially, because of the inordinate burden which would be placed on his retentive abilities. It is generally advisable to provide an opportunity for the child to discuss his ideas first, guiding him towards a simple yet satisfactory written statement of them. Thus at Stage 1 his story may well be no more than a brief sentence. A young child may wish also to illustrate his story. This adds to his pleasure and satisfaction in the total operation and so is reinforcing.
7. It is important that the child's story be typed or 'printed' by the teacher and bound together with the stories of the previous days. Ideally the word learning, the writing and the re-reading of the typed copy of the material is accomplished within a twenty-four hour period. Frequently scheduled re-readings throughout the day further reinforce learning and accelerate progress. As the collection of stories grows, in book form, this provides tangible proof of progress for the child who so badly needs to experience success.
8. The child's retention of 'learned' words in his word file is checked regularly so that provision can be made for re-learning where necessary and progress can be systematically evaluated.

Stage 3. This stage is achieved when the needed word is presented to the child in printed form and from merely looking at it, while saying it, he is enabled to write it from memory. He now no longer needs to have the word written for him nor does he need to trace it prior to writing it himself. The child gradually develops the ability to learn words of even four or five syllables by saying them as he glances over them once or twice and then writing them from memory. As always, the words are needed words, deriving from his own experience and posing no comprehension difficulty.

At this stage too, the child usually begins to want to read books. He is allowed to choose whatever interests him (at an appropriate reading level) and he is told the words he does not recognise. When the reading of a particular story or selection is completed, the new words are gone over and written by the child, after the manner described above.

Three basic principles must be observed:

(a) The words to be learned are never copied,
(b) Each word is always written as a whole,
(c) Attention is always directed to meanings as the child is now meeting words some of which may be outside his oral vocabulary.

Stage 4. At this stage the child acquires the ability to recognise new words from their similarity to words or parts of words already learned. Soon after the child has begun to learn directly from the printed word, he begins to generalise and to make out new words from their resemblance to words or syllables he already knows. Usually by now too, the child is eager to read. He is encouraged to read about anything that is of interest to him. It is crucial that the material be of high interest value to the child so that he will be motivated to complete the reading in order to gain particular information or to follow the course of an exciting story.

At this level of competence, the child has no great difficulty in writing his own stories or reports within the context of his current reading level.

Evaluative Comments on the Technique

1. The Fernald technique is essentially a remedial technique, for use with severely disabled readers.
2. It is time-consuming and for that reason is used usually when the child has failed to make progress with other remedial techniques. Furthermore its use requires a one-to-one tutoring situation.
3. The teacher may expect to find the learner very slow in showing any measurable improvement during Stage 1. It is necessary to be extremely patient and to persevere, remembering that the child on this programme is usually one who has been unsuccessful in using other remedial techniques. Consequently, he is unlikely to find the initially slow progress tedious.
4. The Fernald technique is easily initiated in any one-to-one remedial situation, as there are no costly materials or hardware used.

Possible Secondary Gains

1. For the child who has had a long history of reading failure, the Fernald technique provides a fresh and different approach which ensures success, however limited, even in the initial stages. The child's attitude to reading is usually improved as a result of this and there is an enhancement of his self-concept.
2. There is strong emphasis on reading for meaning, as it is through the use of the child's own stories – the language experience approach – that the initial competence is built up. Good reading comprehension is fostered by this practice.
3. In finger-tracing the words, the child learns the correct formation of letters and their correct spatial sequencing in words. This is of particular help to the child with mixed laterality, who may be experiencing some difficulty in establishing the correct orientation of words.
4. Through using the Fernald technique the child masters spellings as an integral part of the whole process and he becomes familiar with the probable sequencing of letters in

words.

5. Not infrequently, the handwriting of the child taught by this method, improves considerably. This technique promotes regularity of handwriting and it helps to eradicate faulty practices that the child may have previously acquired.
6. The hyperactive child who has a very short attention span, is helped by the finger-tracing procedure. This technique provides a motor outlet for his energies and channels his attention to the task in hand. This fosters in him the ability to be selectively attentive and thus lays the foundation for good study habits.

References

1. Fernald, G.M. *Remedial Techniques in Basic School Subjects.* New York: McGraw-Hill Book Co., 1943.
2. Peters, M.L. *Spelling: Caught or Taught?* London: Routledge and Kegan Paul, 1967.
3. Montessori, M. *The Montessori Method.* New York: Frederick A. Stokes, 1912.

5. *Assessment of Teacher Competence in Reading Instruction*

William W. Anderson, Shippensburg State College, Pennsylvania

Each of us has his or her own idea as to what a "really good" teacher of reading is like. In most instances, however, this is little more than an elusive and fuzzy concept. Simple though it may be to compile a string of adjectives that seems to fit good teachers of reading, it is quite another matter to objectively measure teacher competence. Because reading pedagogy is concerned with improvement of a process rather than subject-matter content, measurement is especially difficult and complex.

The possibility of measuring the competence of reading teachers suggests a number of questions. Can the attitudes and skills necessary for optimally effective reading instruction be measured? Are there uniquely different factors found in the exceptionally capable teacher of reading that are not present in the "really good" teacher in the general sense? What tools might be useful in assisting the conscientious teacher to discover strengths and weaknesses in reading pedagogy? Are there better ways than the typical college test or informal observation for teacher educators to identify potentially weak teachers of reading or problem areas in their preparation? These questions are fruitful areas for research and adequate answers would likely result in significant improvements in the quality of reading instruction.

The purpose of this paper is to synthesise research findings pertaining to the above questions with special emphasis upon identifying and reviewing useful measurement tools.

Existing Research and Practice

The literature concerning prediction of teacher competence in reading pedagogy reveals extensive research on this subject.[1,2,3,4,5,6,7,8] Yet, with a few notable exceptions, this research has been focused upon knowledge of phonics and other word attack skills. As valuable as this type of research may be, it does not provide a means for measurement of the qualities that are most essential for the optimally effective teacher of reading.

The most difficult problem in assessing competence of teachers of reading has been in the determination of an appropriate criterion. A symposium of specialists gathered for the National Reading Conference in Houston, Texas, in 1973 to investigate teacher competence in reading pedagogy could not even produce agreement on the characteristics that a "master" teacher of reading possesses.[9] If there is, however, one criterion variable that the greatest number of reading professionals might be expected to agree upon, it is reasonable to assume that it would be professional information or knowledge of the subject matter of reading pedagogy. Though it is frequently observed that knowledge does not insure practice, yet practice is unlikely without knowledge. Several researchers have suggested that this variable is most useful and most amenable to measurement.[2,9,10]

Erroneous conclusions concerning teacher competence in reading pedagogy frequently have their roots in fallacious reasoning of two extreme types. On the one hand, many administractors have been prone to infer teacher competence from the improvement in test scores of students taught by that teacher. Student gains on standardized reading achievement tests have all too commonly been viewed as a direct reflection of the quality of instruction provided. Of all the classic, correlation-causation traps of education, this one must rank among the most pernicious. Those espousing this simplistic view maintain that the "proof of the pudding" is most logically found in student performance. Despite the consternation of misjudged teachers and reading professionals, this unfortunate and specious type of assessment practice still persists. A contrasting, though almost equally fallacious, view of teacher assessment in reading is that which gives unwarranted weight to grades achieved in college courses. Hopefully, the grades assigned in college reading courses do have some predictive validity for classroom performance. Nevertheless, they obviously leave much unsaid concerning the prospective teacher's ability to interact with children. As helpful as such predictive indices may be, they do not reflect one's ability to organise, to implement and to transfer competencies learned in the controlled and artificial world of academia to the "real world" of the classroom. It is reasonable to assume that grades are more predictive of performance in direct correspondence to the quality of the real experiences that are included in their determination. Nevertheless, even the best pre-professional field experiences are substantially removed from the long-term demands and responsibilities to be assumed by the practicing professional.

Representative Assessment Instruments

There are several instruments that are especially noteworthy for the measurement of professional information possessed by in-service and pre-service teachers of reading. Two of these will be reviewed below and others that may be of value will be cited with brief annotations.

Artley, A. and Hardin, V. Inventory of Teacher Knowledge of Reading *(Revised Edition). Columbia, Missouri: Lucas Brothers Publishers, 1975.*
Artley and Hardin's Inventory is probably the most valid and comprehensive of the various instruments available for the measurement of professional information about reading pedagogy. Moreover, it is the only one of recent vintage that purports to measure the whole spectrum of teacher knowledge concerning reading instruction.

The inventory consists of 97 multiple-choice items with four possible responses for each item. It is self-administering and there are no time limits.

Items are drawn from seven areas that the authors believe to be consistently treated in reading methods texts. These areas are: the reading act, preparation for reading, word identification, comprehension and critical reading, reading in the content areas, reading interests and tastes, and corrective procedures. Factor analysis did not show these areas to be identifiable as discrete factors. Nevertheless, the procedure for item selection does guarantee adequate coverage of professional information generally recognized as important for reading teachers.

The items included in the Inventory were chosen from among those checked by a "representative group of reading specialists" as valid and important "bits" of professional information. Revision and rewriting was then undertaken based upon the reaction and comments made by this group. This revised Inventory was then administered to a heterogeneous group of 552 practicing elementary classroom teachers. The resulting data were analysed and those items having low reliability were removed.

The authors suggest several caveats that should be observed. First, they note that factor analysis does not justify diagnostic use of the inventory and therefore the score should be interpreted simply as a global measure of understanding. Secondly, they emphasize that in no way does this measure indicate the extent to which the teacher might use these understandings in the classroom.

Since the Inventory was not intended for comparative use, no norms are included. Establishment of local norms is suggested if base-line information is desired. The Kingston, Brosier, Hsu validation study and review of the original edition[9] cites this as a shortcoming. It might rather be construed, however, as a tribute to Artley and Hardin's recognition of the inherent limitations and dangers of using such an instrument comparatively.

The Inventory has value for individual and group assessment of specific deficits despite its failure to hold up under the rigours of factor analysis. It is an outstanding tool for research and has much to recommend it in spite of its several shortcomings, the most notable of which is the lack of an adequate manual. Some may find it helpful to use the Inventory as Dr. Artley reports that he does, as a final examination in basic methods courses and as a means of discovering areas and topics that need to be given additional emphasis in subsequent courses.

Durkin, D. Phonics Test for Teachers. *New York: Teachers College Press, Columbia University, 1964.*
Designed especially for use in reading methods courses, this test is "to help teachers and student teachers identify what they do and do not know about phonics." It is also a self-administering instrument with no time limit, but the author states that administration and checking will generally require about 45 minutes.

The test is divided into ten parts as follows: syllabication, vowels: long and short, vowel generalisations, sounds of *oo*, sounds of *qu*, and sounds of *x*. Phonics content that was considered to be either too easy (e.g. regular consonant sounds) or too technical was omitted. The items included represent minimal information that should be known by every elementary classroom teacher. Beyond this comment, there is no further information provided in the brief manual concerning the development of test items, validation procedures, statistical analyses, etc.

No norms are provided. There is, however, a group summary sheet with instructions for tallying responses to identify areas of weakness.

The test has several serious shortcomings. The two most obvious have to do with the nature of responses required for testing knowledge of different phonics generalisations and with the inconsistent number of items used in the various parts of the test. For example, knowledge of the two different sounds of *oo* is tested by asking the examinee to produce these sounds, whereas the same type of knowledge for *qu* is tested on a recognition basis. Also, some segments of phonic knowledge are tested using as many as sixteen items whereas others have as few as two items as a basis for the same type of conclusion. If all items were cast in the same form, requiring the same level of cognitive response, a more nearly valid indication of phonic knowledge could be expected.

In summary, though this test has value as a diagnostic and instructional tool for basic reading methods courses and in-service programs, the same type of information could be obtained as well by a locally prepared test or one of several criterion-type phonics tests included as part of self-instructional test.

Narang, H.L. "Self-Evaluation of a Reading Lesson for Reading Teachers." Elementary English, *52: 338-339, March, 1975.*
This simple checklist is based on the Directed Reading Activity. It is divided into five sections as follows: objectives, readiness and motivation, development, review and follow-up. The user responds to a series of questions such as: "Was the silent reading guided?" or, "Was the reading done for a purpose?" This type of checklist might be useful for micro-teaching, student teachers, or other beginners. It may also have value as a counselling tool for supervisors of beginning teachers.

Aaron, et al. Conducting In-Service Programs in Reading. *Newark Delaware: International Reading Association, 1965, 46 pp.*
This little handbook is one of the highly practical Reading Aids Series. It includes five survey forms or checklists that are helpful in pinpointing strengths and weaknesses relating to several dimensions of reading instruction. The format and type of response called for on each checklist are varied. The forms provided are: (a) Instructional Practices in Basal Reading Class, (b) Teacher Beliefs and Practices in the Teaching of Basal Reading, (c) Use of Basal Readers and Related Material, (d) Evaluation of Program, Materials, Equipment, and Practices, and (e) Practices Related to Reading in the Content Areas. These forms may assist teachers in taking stock of their own effectiveness or they may also be helpful to administrators and supervisors in assessing needs for in-service. The experience of completing a survey of this type may, in itself, spark the teacher to reassess his or her practices in teaching reading.

Structured Observations

Rutherford[12] has developed a useful guide for observing reading instruction. It is similar, in many respects, to systems designed for analysis of classroom interaction. Yet it is more specifically applicable to reading instruction in that class time spent in various reading-related activities is categorised, recorded at five second intervals and tabulated as follows: C = Comprehension development, R = Word recognition, O = Oral reading, S =

Silent reading, E = Enrichment activities, L = Listening skills development. Even though this seems to be a rather cumbersome system, it does, nevertheless, have interesting possibilities as a tool for assessing teacher strengths and weaknesses in directing a group reading activity.

Another tool that warrants attention is one developed by Robinson.[13] It differs from Rutherford's Guide in that it is more appropriate for use following a series of observation sessions as a counselling scale for the teacher being observed. It is designed to help teachers see the inter-relationships of reading skills and to facilitate integrated teaching. It consists of seven questions, each covering a broad area of concern in reading instruction. Questions cover all major skill aspects of reading instruction as Robinson perceives them.[14] Beneath each question a number of related concerns are listed. For example: "Does instruction promote the various aids to readiness for reading and word perception and provide for their development?________ auditory discrimination, ________visual discrimination,________ meaning clues,________work form clues,________details of form ________phonetic analysis, ________ structural analysis,________use of dictionary."

Summary

Reading professionals who are interested in, or responsible for, the assessment of teacher competence and who wish to insure some level of objectivity might possibly find all of the instruments cited above to be unsuitable for use in their specific situations. Nevertheless, they do provide a point of departure from which locally prepared instruments can be developed that will more nearly approach objectivity. Endeavours of this type are most worthwhile in that they preclude the use of completely subjective, informal assessment procedures that are frequently arbitrary, indefensible and unprofessional. Measurement of teacher effectiveness in reading pedagogy is a task that should command far greater attention than it has yet been given. The potential benefits for children and their teachers are too great to go unheeded.

References and Bibliography

1. Aaron, I.E., Callaway B. and Olson, A.V. *Conducting In-Service Programs in Reading.* Newark, Del.: International Reading Association, 1965.
2. Artley, A. and Hardin, V. *Inventory of Teacher Knowledge of Reading* (Rev. ed.). Columbia, Mo.: Lucas Brothers Publishers, 1975.
3. Broman, B. Factors Associated with Teacher Knowledge of Reading Skills. *Dissertation Abstracts*, 1962, *23*, 1966.
4. Durkin, D. *Phonics Test for Teachers.* New York: Teachers College Press, Columbia University, 1964.
5. Ilika, J. Phonic Skills of Teacher Education Students. In G.B. Schick and M.M. May (Eds.), *Multidisciplinary Aspects of College-Adult Reading* (Seventeenth Yearbook of the National Reading Conference). Milwaukee, Wis.: National Reading Conference, 1968.
6. Mazurkiewicz, A. What the Professor Doesn't Know About Phonics Can Hurt! *Reading World,* 1975, *15*, 65-86.
7. Narang, H. Self-Evaluation of a Reading Lesson for Reading Teachers. *Elementary English*, 1975, *52*, 338-9.
8. Schubert, D. Teachers and Word Analysis Skills. *Journal of Developmental Reading*, 1959, *2*, 62-4.
9. Kingston, A., Brosier, G.F. and Hsu, Y.M. The Inventory of Teacher Knowledge of Reading – A Validation. *Reading Teacher*, 1975, *29*, 133-6.
10. Miller, C. and Miller, D. The Importance of Certain Personal Qualities and Professional Competencies in Successful Classroom Teaching. *Journal of Teacher Education*, 1971, *32*, 37-9.
11. Wilson, R. and Hall, M. *Programmed Word Attack for Teachers* (2nd ed.) Columbus, Ohio: Charles E. Merrill Publishers, 1975.
12. Rutherford, W. An Analysis of Teacher Effectiveness in Classroom Instruction in Reading. In N.B. Smith (Ed.), *Reading Methods and Teacher Improvement.* Newark, Del.: International Reading Association, 1971.
13. Robinson, H. Sample Questions to consider in Appraising the Scope and Adequacy of Reading Programs. (Mimeographed form prepared for NDEA Institute; 1967), pp. 4-5.
14. Whipple, G. A Modern Reading Program for This Season. In T.R. Carlson (Ed.), *Administrators and Reading.* New York: Harcourt, Brace, Jovanovich; 1972.
15. Hahn, H. What is Needed in In-Service Education? In P.C. Berg and J.E. George (Eds.), *Current Administrative Problems in Reading.* Newark, Del.: International Reading Association, 1968.
16. Rorie, I. Analysis and Validation of the Inventory of Teacher Knowledge of Reading (Doctoral dissertation, University of Missouri, 1975, University Microfilms No. 76-1041).
17. Wade, E. The Construction and Validation of a Test of Ten Teacher Skills Used in Reading Instruction, Grades 2-5. (Doctoral dissertation, Indiana University, 1960). *Dissertation Abstracts*, 1960, *22*, 167-8.

II. LEARNING TO READ

6. *Comprehending Comprehension: Classroom Implications*

George Livingstone, Hamilton College of Education, Scotland

Lewin once said "there is nothing so practical as good theory." I believe that and I was reminded of it the other day when, for the first time (to my face), I was called "a theorist." I don't think it was meant as an insult but I had to think about it before deciding that it was probably a back-handed compliment. It served to remind me of that most unfortunate of all educational dichotomies – that chasm between theory and practice which exists or seems to exist, or which is created for whatever purpose. The dichotomy is as pertinent in the field of the teaching of reading as it would seem to be elsewhere in education. In this paper I hope above all else to bridge the gap, to marry theory to practice, to show how they can be brought together.

Fuelling my endeavours are two very basic beliefs – when a teacher understands what she is doing and why, the effectiveness of her teaching is improved. In other words, understanding the nature of what is to be taught will provide necessary guidance and structure to her teaching. Associated with this belief is another which I hold just as firmly. I believe that what can be learned ought to be taught; things which can be learned ought to be taught and not left to whim or chance. These two beliefs mean that in the field of the teaching of reading I hold that there are certain key concepts about the nature of the reading process (the theory) which are worth understanding, are understandable in practical terms and which will guide the development of programmes of teaching. The ultimate test of the theory is for me in terms of its operability in classrooms.

I fully realise the breadth of the task to be encompassed within this one paper but believe that the effort is very necessary and potentially very useful. The structure of this paper will therefore be firstly to examine the fundamental nature of the reading process, then to move on to look at certain key linking concepts (between theory and practice), thence to proceed to list the needs of the effective reader (the objectives of a reading programme) and finally to recommend practices which would attain these objectives and mention relevant materials.

What is Reading?

Depending on the answer to this question is the fate of all else which follows. Examination of "the literature" reveals wide variations in the answers to this question. In the diagram which follows, imagine that the three squares are, in fact, a series of overlays which have simply been prised apart for purposes of dissection only. In reality they are interconnected and almost inextricable one from the other.

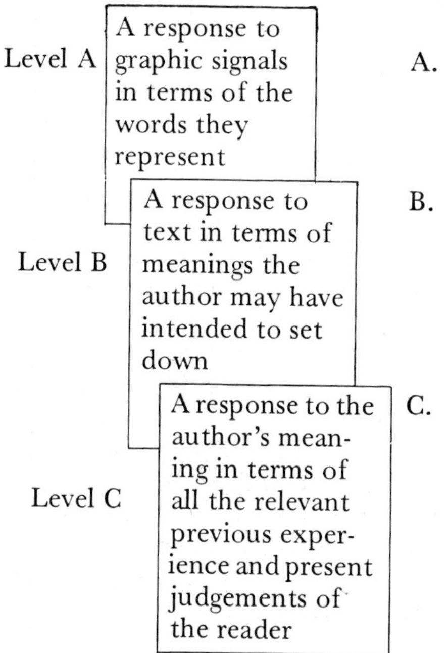

A. "Reading is a series of word perceptions." (Spache)

B. "Reading is a complex process by which the reader reconstructs, to some degree, a message encoded in graphic language." (Goodman)

C. "Reading involves the same sort of organisation and analytic action as occurs in thinking of higher sorts." (Thorndike)

What answers does this diagram present?

1 Reading involves a response to text. "To read is to respond" (Bullock). The response always involves the striving for comprehension. *Reading is comprehension or understanding.* Reading is, thus, thinking in the context of reading.
2 Reading is *not* a simple process of graphic (visual) input and phonological output. Reading is a complex network of interrelated skills and experiences. It is a "mental" activity, not solely one of visual perception.
3 There are, however, different levels (or phases) involved in the act of reading. These levels are not in any real way discrete. Reading is a holistic rather than a molecular response to text.

Which Concepts Make This Definition Operable?

To realise that reading is comprehending and thus involves thinking is important. To act upon such realisation is another matter. Fortunately there are several key concepts and important findings which can provide a framework for classroom operability.

Firstly, there are the taxonomies of Bloom[1] and of Barrett.[2] Bloom's Taxonomy (Cognitive Domain) is concerned with levels of learning tasks generally. Barrett's work is more specific to reading and is based on the notion of the level of thinking required to make a full response to any reading task. Basically Barrett identifies four such levels of comprehension (literal; reorganisational; inferential and evaluative). Whilst these taxonomies are both hypothetical constructs, they are very useful and practical (Bloom has also been supported by some research findings). The notion of level of thinking involved in reading tasks is a thoroughly serviceable organising principle. It runs throughout all that follows.

Secondly, there are various research findings from the field of developmental psychology. In the area of thinking we are familiar with Piaget's developmental stages in thinking. In terms of these stages one would expect that children of primary school age would, in the main, be capable of coping only with the first two of Barrett's levels (literal and reorganisational). Certainly, the majority of readers in schools seem to coincide with such a notion! Peel has some findings in the area of reading which would seem to support the notion that it is not until the age of 13 or 14 years that children are capable of dealing properly with ideas which involve competing possibilities and probabilities rather than those which involve the here and now. Whilst acknowledging the importance of such findings, there are cautionary notes to be added. In the first place, such findings do not mean that *only* 13 or 14 year olds can cope with such matters (nor do they mean that all 13/14 year old can do so). Such an interpretation of developmental stages is far too rigid to be realistic; it also goes well beyond Piaget's intent. When Piaget's work is examined directly, it can be seen that his model of learning is an interaction model and this means that development takes place by interaction between learner and environment. In other words, development occurs through learners moving on from their existing predominant stage towards "the other stages" (the basic concept of dissonance applies). From this interpretation and from my own experience, children *throughout the primary school* can cope with all of Barrett's levels, though certain caveats on reader, task and text have to be borne in mind. This point will be resumed in the next set of linking concepts.

Before going on to the final set of concepts, it may be worthwhile summarising what has been said so far.

1 Reading is comprehending and is a complex process.
2 The notion of levels of comprehension can usefully be applied as an organising principle.
3 These levels of comprehending (thinking) must not be seen as strictly sequential, discrete entities. Instead, they reflect a change of emphasis or balance in the reading tasks.

The final set of concepts incorporates the caveats mentioned above and primarily concerns those elements involved in the different levels of comprehension of textual materials. These four elements are, reader, purpose, task (or question) and text. A great deal of what has been written and said about the teaching of reading has fallen into the trap of examining only one of these elements. For example, readability formulae measure, to a degree, the difficulty of the text, but such measures are meaningless unless one considers the reader, the purpose and the task. Difficulty really results from an interaction of reader, purpose, task and text. A look at the permutations of reader, purpose, task and text which occur even in the following brief lists will reveal the need to look at these elements in a holistic way.

Reader	*Purpose*	*Task*	*Text*
Student 9-year old Businessman Joiner	Pass time Pass an exam Find information Appreciation	Discuss Write about Make notes Report on	Newspaper Paperback Learned journal or report Magazine

Thus, the joiner might read the newspaper to find information in order to write it down. The 9-year old child might read the paperback in order to appreciate it and discuss it in class. The list also gives an indication as to what readers may be required to be able to do. In other words, it reveals the elements which have to be considered within the reading programme and which the teacher has to be able to vary to meet these needs fully.

Before going on to the needs of the effective reader I would wish to stress two very important linked issues arising from this list. The importance of establishing appropriate purposes for reading – and setting tasks appropriate to these purposes – cannot be overstated. Some recent findings[3] reveal how even mature, intelligent readers are much less effective than they might be because of a blinkered conception of what was required in reading. Many proved capable of reading only for recall of detail! Treatment did prove to be at least partly effective in these cases. A very important message for teachers!

What the Effective Reader Needs To Be Able To Do

(a) Recognise words and combine them fluently and with speed.

(b) Recognise and comprehend increasingly lengthier and more complex units of meaning.
(c) Cope with the demands of reading at different rates for different purposes.
(d) Cope with the demands of comprehending meaning in various print contexts (both in and out of school).
(e) Cope with the demands of obtaining at levels beyond the literal or manifest in different contexts.
(f) Understand the strategies he uses in his reading.
(g) Understand that reading is a source of pleasure and personal fulfilment.

My own experience and information from recent studies and surveys suggests that schools cope fairly well with (a) and (b), and beyond that the adequacy of teaching declines appreciably. Greater effort is required; renewed understanding of needs is necessary; more thorough examinations of reading programmes are vital; different materials and levels of provision are inescapable. The task of meeting these needs rests ultimately with the teacher. Perhaps the greater present deficit occurs at (g). How often do we see children who *can* read [at least in terms of (a) and (b)] but who *don't* read?

So, to meet these needs, variety of practices and activities is required and more extensive reading materials are essential.

Appropriate Practices and Materials

Throughout all of these suggestions there is the overriding need to have children "respond with alertness" in a variety of ways and in varied groupings.

(i) Individual/group reading to improve skills at literal and reorganisational levels (reading laboratories, basal readers, etc.).
(ii) Group reading and discussion of passages with tasks (questions) which are designed to take children beyond the literal level of comprehension – with teacher involvement.
(iii) Supported individual reading of fiction – at all levels.
(iv) Group reading and discussion of shared reading of fiction – with teacher involved.

(v) Group reading and discussion of prediction exercises – with teacher involved.
(vi) Individual/group work on learning how to process factual information in the contexts of projects or topics – teacher-organised.
(vii) Class listening to and discussing a book read to them by the teacher.

Obviously, not all of these would occur all of the time. What is important is that each receive its due place in the programme. The practices outlined could become a skeleton upon which a check-list of provision could be based. The centrality of the teacher is clear, as is the need for good planning and organisation on a school-wide basis. Only by good practice can good theory become effective.

One final point is worth making and it refers not only to the practices above, but to the overall theory. Reading is one aspect of a language programme. Obvious and intentionally included in the list of practices above are other aspects of language work. Such a reading programme would mean that the various aspects of language (reading, speaking, writing, listening) come together meaningfully and link effectively.

Summary

1 Reading is thinking, i.e. the striving to comprehend.
2 Comprehension can take different forms and levels. This notion is important in guiding practice.
3 Reading is a holistic act. Cognisance must be taken of all elements comprising the totality.
4 Effective readers need to be able to undertake a variety of tasks.
5 Practices must reflect the needs of the effective reader.

References

1. Bloom, B.S., Englehart, M.D., Furst, E.J., Hill, W.H. and Krathwohl, D.R. *A taxonomy of educational objectives I.* London: Longman, 1956.
2. Barrett, T.C. Taxonomy of cognitive and affective dimensions of reading comprehension. In Robinson, H.M. (Ed.). *Innovation and change in reading instruction.* Chicago: University of Chicago Press, 1968.
3. Marton, F. and Saljo, R. On qualitative differences in learning. *British Journal of Educational Psychology, 46,* 4-11, 1976 and 46, 115-27, 1976.
4. Goodman, K. In Harris L.A. and Smith, C.B. *Individualising reading instruction: a reader.* New York: Holt, Rinehart and Winston, 1972.
5. Peel, E.A. The analysis of comprehension and judgment from textual material. *Education Review,* Vol. 27, No. 2, February, 1975.
6. Great Britain, Department of Education and Science *A language for life.* (The Bullock Report) London: H.M.S.O., 1975.
7. Spache, G. *Reading in the elementary school.* Boston: Allyn and Bacon, 1964.
8. Thorndike, E.L. Reading as reasoning: A study of mistakes in paragraph reading. *Journal of Educational Psychology,* June, 1917.

7. *On the Differential Transfer of Abilities to Reading*

Fred W. Ohnmacht and James T. Fleming, State University of New York at Albany

The purpose of this paper is to consider the question of which individual difference variables have transfer value at various stages of learning reading skills, ranging from those characterising acquisition at early stages of learning to read, to later more facile and mature stages of reading development. In general we take the position that different abilities or skills serve to differentiate normal readers from their poorer reading peers at various reading levels. Put in another way, abilities which discriminate normal from poor readers who are reading at a first grade level are not the same as those which would serve the same function for say readers at the third grade level. In turn discriminating variables at the third grade level are likely to be different than those found at the sixth or seventh grade level.[1]

Learning and abilities

First, consider some early work which has done much to shape our thinking in these matters. In two seminal papers, Ferguson proposed a broad scheme drawing together, within a single conceptual framework, the study of human learning and the study of human ability.[2, 3] Abilities are considered to be the result of over-learning of patterns of processing information as evidenced by behaviour which when overlearned becomes more or less invariant and at least a crude limit of performance is reached. The second important aspect of Ferguson's theory concerns the role of abilities, as thus defined, in subsequent learning. Here, the question of the transfer of abilities to subsequent learning is at issue and more importantly, for our purposes, it is suggested that the abilities which transfer and produce their effects at one stage of learning may be different from those which transfer at later stages of learning. Indeed, Fleishman has repeatedly demonstrated this to be the case when the acquisition of various psychomotor skills is studied.[4] He has found that the abilities relevant to acquisition of skill early in a learning skill are *not* the same abilities which transfer at terminal stages of learning.

Abilities and Transfer

A model of learning and transfer based on a conception of hierarchical learning sets has been presented by Gagné.[5] For Gagné, a complex learning outcome is dependent on subordinate capabilities referred to as learning sets with any set possibly itself having several subordinate learning sets itself, thus the hierarchical nature of the model. Subordinate learning sets are viewed as mediating positive transfer to learning sets above them in a postulated network and this is termed vertical transfer. Lateral transfer has to do with the broadening application of a learning set in a variety of situations. Importantly, the learning sets at the bottom of a hierarchy are fundamental human capabilities which are immediately relevant to various contiguous learning sets. These fundamental capabilities are in part a function of prior learning, and in part a function of development (i.e. maturation of visual receptors and the like). Learning sets higher in a hierarchy are those sets implicated as being particularly relevant to the task to be learned as a function of a sequence of instruction. Of course, there are points of contact here with Ferguson's theory. Early in life fundamental abilities due to maturation unfold and make a contribution to the attainment of other abilities through the interaction of the individual with his environment. Abilities are those human capacities which have reached their crude limit of performance or learning. If one seeks to instruct someone, subsequent learning sets (for example how to read) must be imparted and the basic abilities mediate transfer to these sets. To make progress, subordinate sets must be mastered before super-ordinate sets may be accomplished. In one sense then each subordinate set must be overlearned to become, in Ferguson's terms, an ability, which in conjunction with more basic abilities mediate transfer to higher levels. Failure to acquire subordinate set mastery or more fundamentally to reach sufficiently high levels of performance on the most fundamental abilities might result in a cumulative deficit for the learner as super-ordinate learning sets are encountered in an instructional sequence due to an inadequate basis for mediating transfer to higher levels.

With the foregoing as a basis for organisation let us consider several examples from the literature which suggest that the differential transfer of abilities to reading at various stages of reading development is a reasonably satisfactory model. Consider visual perceptual variables. At an early stage (say before age 5); such variables are in a state of flux and changing rapidly as a function of maturation and learning. Over time these variables begin to assume the role of abilities in Ferguson's terms since most children reach stable levels of performance. Of course, the age at which such stability is attained may very well vary from child to child and from ability to ability. But beyond this, it is interesting to note that visual perception variables are more strongly related to gross terminal reading performance at the end of grade one and there is a decrement when the criterion is performance at the end of subsequent grades.[6, 7] This very general observation can be viewed as a function of differential transfer.

Of course, the reason for such a state of affairs is open to differential interpretation. Rourke[8] has summarised a number of studies which at this point may be viewed at least in part as supporting his (and others') contention that cerebral dysfunction due to brain damage plays a role in reading retardation while at the same time providing support for hypotheses relating to the changing nature of deficits responsible for reading retardation with advancing age which spring from a developmental lag position.[9, 10] The types of studies summarised by Rourke[8] and Satz *et al*,[9] suggest that within a typical group of disabled readers at least two sub-groups can be identified. One sub-group's deficits are attributable to impaired left or right cerebral dysfunction due to damage, whereas the other group's dysfunction is due to a lag in the maturation of the brain which delays the acquisition of skills important to early phases of reading (e.g. differentiating graphic symbols and the like). This is quite consistent with the observation of De Hirsch, Jansky, and Langford[11] that about half of an observed group of poor first grade readers subsequently made improvement while the rest continued to fail.

Interestingly Brittain[12] found that the ability to apply morphological rules demonstrated an increasing relationship with reading achievement over grades 1 and 2 which is consistent with the notion that as children mature, variables which differentiate normal from poor readers begin to reflect linguistic processes. Some of the author's own work[13] suggests that by second grade, normal readers tend to encode words on the basis of their semantic features whereas their poorer reading peers are dominated by the phonemic features of a word. By sixth grade these differences are notable by their absence. As another case in point, children's ability to utilise super-ordinate taxonomic categories to organise retrieval of word lists from memory makes an increasing contribution to the prediction of reading achievement during the early years of schooling.[14] Indeed, at a more reductionistic level, Kinsbourne[15] reports differential transfer of presumed specific reading component tasks to reading performance over relatively short periods of time during initial instruction in reading (6 to 9 months).

Word-bounding and reading achievement

A recent study by a student at the State University of New York[16] points to additional complexities. He studied the rate of development of the ability to bound words employing six-word boundary recognition tasks, three each in the modalities of speech and print. Further he evaluated the validity of each task to predict reading achievement at the end of kindergarten, grade 1 and grade 2. He found rates of development and their trends varied among the tasks over the age range studied and that at any grade level the tasks exhibited a degree of independence which suggested that the ability to bound words is not a unitary ability at the grade levels studied. He also noted that the word boundary tasks continued to make non-trivial contributions to the prediction of end-of-year reading achievement, but that the task or tasks contributing to the prediction, changed from grade to grade! Thus, even when considering a particular ability such as word bounding it is quite possible to identify variants in task requirements which identify facets of the ability, which develop differentially and themselves demonstrate empirical patterns consistent with a differential transfer model.

Conclusion

In summary, given the strong case which can be made for differential transfer of abilities to reading, it follows that no one phenomenon – no one etiological explanation – can account clearly and persuasively, at any one stage of development for children's difficulties in learning to read. These days one might assume this to be a truism, and yet Vernon[17] currently claims that, in her words, an "incorrect assumption still (is) held by many . . . that the cause of reading difficulties is unitary; that is, that all reading problems arise from a single inherent deficiency that is the same in all poor readers." In her concise manner of treating the topic of varieties of deficiency in the reading processes she reminds us that, once again in her words, ". . . it should be evident that little will be gained if disabled readers are regarded as a homogeneous group."[17] We take her words to be a compatible echo of our position which also suggests that while none are sufficiently explanatory, equally no one phenomenon or etiological explanation should be ruled out – out of hand – as a potential source of children's difficulties in learning to read.

References

1. Ohnmacht, F.W. Individual differences and reading. In Schick, G. and May, M. (eds.) *Reading: Research and pedagogy*. Milwaukee, Wisconsin: National Reading Conference, 1970 pp. 242-47.
2. Ferguson, G.A. On learning and human ability. *Canadian Journal of Psychology*, 1954, 8, 95-112.
3. Ferguson, G.A. On transfer and the abilities of man. *Canadian Journal of Psychology*, 1956, 10, 121-31.

4. Fleishman, E.A. Individual differences and motor learning. In Gagné, R.M. *Learning and individual differences*, Columbus, Ohio: Merrill, 1967, pp. 165-91.
5. Gagné, R.M. Cognitive structure in material to be learned. *Psychological Review*, 1962, 69, 355-65.
6. Goins, J.T. *Visual perceptual abilities and early reading progress.* Supplementary Educational Monographs, No. 87, Chicago: University of Chicago Press, 1958.
7. Rosen, C. and Ohnmacht, F.W. Perception, readiness, and reading achievement in first grade. In Smith H. (ed.) *Perception and reading,* Newark, Delaware, International Reading Association, 1967, pp. 33-8.
8. Rourke, B.P. Brain-behaviour relationships in children with learning disabilities: a research program. *American Psychologist,* 1975, 30, 911-20.
9. Satz, P., Friel, J. and Rudegeair, F. Some predictive antecedents of specific reading disability: a two-, three-, and four-year follow up. In Guthrie, J.T. (ed.) *Aspects of reading acquisition.* Baltimore, Maryland: Johns Hopkins Press, 1976. pp. 111-40.
10. Satz, P., Rardin, D. and Ross, J. an Evaluation of a theory of developmental dyslexia. *Child Development,* 1971, 42, 2009-21.
11. DeHirsch, K., Jansky, J., and Langford, W. *Predicting reading failure.* New York: Harper and Row, 1966.
12. Brittain, M. Inflectional performance and early reading. *Reading Research* Quarterly, 1970, 6, 34-8.
13. Ohnmacht, F.W. and Fleming, J.T. Developmental changes in memory attributes of good and poor readers. In McNinch, G. and Millen, W. *Reading: convention and inquiry.* Clemson, South Carolina: National Reading Conference, 1975 pp. 255-62.
14. Ohnmacht, F.W. and Corrado, T. Clustering in free recall: its relationship to reading achievement. (In preparation).
15. Kinsbourne, M. Looking and listening strategies and beginning reading. In Guthrie, J.T. (ed.) *Aspects of reading acquisition,* Baltimore, Maryland: Johns Hopkins University Press, 1976.
16. Warren, B. Chilren's word boundary recognition ability and its relationship to reading. Unpublished doctoral dissertation. Albany, New York: University of New York at Albany, 1977.
17. Vernon, M.D. Varieties of deficiency in reading processes. *Harvard Educational Review*, 1977, 47, 396-410.

8. *Incidence and Correlates of Illiteracy in Irish Primary Schools**

Patricia J. Fontes and Thomas Kellaghan, Educational Research Centre, St. Patrick's College, Dublin.

Problems related to the acquisition by children of skills in reading and writing have frequently been an object of concern in recent years – in the media, among teachers and among members of the general public. Concern has been expressed about the effects of reading and writing disabilities on both pupils' ability to follow school courses and their ability to function in society. As far as school-work is concerned, the problem probably achieved increased visibility in this country with the transfer of an increasing number of pupils to post-primary school and with the raising of the school-leaving age.

Concern with problems of literacy is by no means new nor is it confined to this country. In fact, our current problems are probably small by comparison with those in the past and with those in developing countries. However, contemporary western societies remain conscious of the fact that their problems of literacy cannot be regarded as inconsiderable. While mass education no doubt has contributed to the reduction of such problems, an increase in the information and symbol processing requirements of post-industrial societies means that higher standards of literacy are required today than in the past if one is to function satisfactorily in work and everyday life. Besides, it may be that providing literacy skills for the relatively small

*A copy of this paper has been published in the *Irish Journal of Education,* Vol. 11, Nos. 1 and 2, Summer and Winter 1977, since presentation of the Reading Association of Ireland Conference.

proportion of the population that remains illiterate under conditions of mass education may be a different and more intractable problem than providing such skills for the general population. It is not always appreciated that the modern expectation that nearly everyone should attain a high level of reading skill, enabling them to draw inferential as well as directly stated information from texts, is a new development and poses a unique challenge to contemporary societies and educational system.[1]

What we have said implies that the level of literacy required for functioning in society may vary from time to time and according to the demands of one's occupation. It is not surprising then that definitions of literacy in the literature vary; a single definition which would apply to all people of all ages in all countries and at all stages of economic development would not be possible. In an historical review, Resnick and Resnick[1] concluded that when the standard of literacy set is rather low (e.g., to read aloud a simple and well-known passage) one can expect a high incidence of literacy, while when the standard set is high (as when one must be able to read unfamiliar texts and obtain new information from them), relatively smaller numbers of people attain literacy.

Approaches to the definition and measurement of literacy may be categorised broadly under two headings. Firstly, there are those approaches which focus on functioning in daily life. Thus, for example, in Britain, literacy has been defined as being "able to read and write for practical purposes of daily life".[2] In the United States, a rather similar definition was operationalised in terms of competence in specific reading tasks; for example, "to read and understand all sections of a newspaper, with particular emphasis on the classified and advertisement section; to read and understand voter registration instructions; to read labels or such household items as groceries, recipes, medicine instructions; to read materials necessary to perform jobs; to read personal letters, bills."[3]

Side by side with such definitions based on functioning in daily life, educational criteria of literacy have also been widely used. The most frequently used criteria of this kind have been length of education or performance on standardised tests. In most cases, the standardised tests have been norm-referenced, and a score below a certain reading age (commonly seven years) has been used as an index of illiteracy.

In this paper, we shall look at measures of literacy that can broadly be defined as both functional and educational. Our concern is with the reading and writing abilities of children at the stage when they are in their last year in primary school. We asked teachers of sixth standard children (aged 11½ to 12½ years) to nominate pupils in their class who were unlikely to be able to cope in their reading and writing (separately), firstly, with the everyday demands of our society, and secondly, with the demands of education in a post-primary school. Certain additional information was also available about the children – their performance on standardised tests of verbal ability and attainment in English, the type of school they were attending, their socio-economic background and ratings of aspects of their behaviour by teachers.

On the basis of this information we propose to examine two issues. Firstly, what is the incidence of the four states of illiteracy as perceived by teachers in the population of sixth-class pupils in Irish schools? And secondly, how do children rated as having literacy problems compare with children not so rated on a number of personal characteristics: verbal ability, standardised test performance in English, socio-economic status and school-related and more general personal-social characteristics?

Method

Sample

The population of Irish national schools (excluding private, Protestant, special and one-teacher schools) was stratified by location (urban-town-rural), size, sex composition and type of administration (religious-lay). Within each stratum, schools were randomly selected. Altogether 128 schools were selected, and these were distributed across the seven sample strata as shown in *Table 8.1*. The total number of national schools in the country in each of the categories represented in the sample is also shown in the table.

In a previously compiled file of pupil information, 3,930 pupils from the schools where all pupils had been rated by their own class teachers and had participated in a testing programme

Table 8.1 *Characteristics of the School Population, the Sample, and the Respondents*

School type	Schools in population	Schools in sample	Sixth standard teachers in sample	Sixth standard pupils in sample	Schools responding In full	Schools responding In part	Sixth standard teachers responding In full	Sixth standard teachers responding In part	Sixth standard pupils rated In full	Sixth standard pupils rated In part
City Boys (4+ teachers)	146	20	52	1,836	12		27		935	
					4**	3	(12)†	4	(429)††	129
City Girls (4+ teachers)	105	18*	40	1,445	13		28		974	
					1**	1	(2)†	2	(100)††	82
Town Boys (4+ teachers)	125	18	33	1,178	12	4	17	5	650	176
Town Girls (4+ teachers)	63	19*	35	1,222	14	3	25	5	884	150
Rural Boys (2-6 teachers)	149	8	8	131	8		8		131	
Rural Girls (2+ teachers)	71	5	5	83	4		4		67	
Rural Mixed (2+ teachers)	2,158	36	36	518	30		30		456	
Subtotal	2,817	124	210	6,413	93	11	139	16	4,097	537
					5**		(14)†		(529)††	
City and town, mixed (3+ teachers)	247	4	4	111	3	0	3	0	102	0
Other	123	0	0	0	0	0	0	0	0	0
Total	3,187	128	214	6,524	96	11	142	16	4,199	537
					5**		(14)†		(529)††	

* One of these schools had no sixth standard class and could not, therefore, respond.

** Schools in which the principal or remedial teacher rated all sixth class pupils.

† The number of teachers represented by a principal or remedial teacher's having rated all sixth-class pupils in schools.

†† The number of sixth-class pupils rated by a principal or remedial teacher instead of by their class teacher.

in the autumn of 1975 were located. These form the base group for the pupil analyses. Correct ages were available for 3,829 of these and ability test scores for 3,512. Because one group of schools did not take the English tests, attainment test results in English were available for only 2,450 of the pupils. Teacher ratings of personal characteristics of pupils were on file for between 3,201 and 3,218 pupils.

Towards the end of the school year 1975-6, field workers were instructed to ask every teacher of sixth class pupils in the selected schools to complete a brief questionnaire about standards of literacy in his/her classroom. Of 214 such teachers in the 126 schools which had sixth classes, ratings were received directly from 158, that is about 74%. These teachers rated a total of 4,736 pupils or 73% of the 6,524 pupils in the school sample.*

For various analyses reported in this paper, different subsets of the total respondent sample were used. One such subset consisted of the schools in which all pupils were rated on literacy by their own class teachers. There were 96 such schools (of the 112 responding) in which 142 teachers rated some 4,199 pupils. Three of these schools were included in only a few analyses because their school type was not intended to be in the sample. Still further subsets consisted of those pupils for whom the various kinds of information besides the teacher ratings were available; this was so in analyses where individual pupils rather than schools were the focus of attention.

Instruments

Literacy Questionnaire The Literacy Questionnaire was a document in which four lists of pupils' names were sought from teachers by directing them as follows:

1 Please name the pupils in your class who, in your opinion, if they were to leave school now, would *not* be able to cope

*In a number of cases, one field worker obtained ratings from principal teachers or from a remedial teacher, instead of from class teachers. An additional 14 teachers were represented by such ratings, bringing the total percentage of classes rated to 80%. Altogether, 529 pupils were rated by their principal or remedial teacher, bringing the total of pupils rated to 81% of the entire pupil sample. Our reported analyses will be confined to ratings made by class teachers, since we cannot be sure that other teachers who rated children used the same standard of judgement as the class teacher.

with the *everyday demands of our society* in
(a) *reading* (e.g., read notices, official forms, newspapers);
(b) in *writing* (e.g., write letters, applications for jobs).

2 Please name the pupils in your class who, in your opinion, would *not* be able to cope with the *demands of education in a post-primary school* (a) in *reading* (e.g., read text-books); (b) in *writing* (e.g., write essays).

Standardised tests The ability test administered was the Drumcondra Verbal Reasoning Test[4] and the test of attainment was the Drumcondra English Test, Level III, Form A.[5] Scores can be derived from the attainment test for reading vocabulary, reading comprehension, total reading (based on a combination of the vocabulary and comprehension subtest scores), language (measuring capitalisation, punctuation, usage, and parts of speech), and spelling.

Ratings of personal characteristics of pupils Ratings on each pupil were obtained on a Pupil Evaluation Form completed by teachers. Each pupil was rated on a five-point scale (5 = very good, 4 = good, 3 = average, 2 = fair, 1 = poor) for the following personal-social characteristics: participation in class, behaviour in school, personal appearance and dress, attention span/concentration, persistence in school work, keenness to get on, speech/use of language, neatness in school work, manners/politeness, getting along with other children, working with limited supervision, and attendance. Teachers were also asked to indicate what kind of post-primary school they considered would be most suitable for each pupil – secondary, vocational, or comprehensive – or whether he/she felt it was still too soon to make such a judgement. Finally, the teacher was asked to state the occupation of the pupil's father or guardian, giving sufficient detail to enable classification of occupational status to be made.

Procedure

The ability and attainment tests were administered to pupils during the first three months of the school year, 1975-6. The tests were administered to the pupils by their own teachers. Around the same time, and before the results of the tests were available to teachers, each teacher was asked to complete a

Pupil Evaluation Form for each pupil in his/her class. The Literacy Questionnaire was administered to teachers towards the end of the school year by a field worker; the questionnaire was completed in the presence of the field worker who was available to give assistance in interpretation.

Incidence of Illiteracy

Since the school was the sampling unit in the study, it was appropriate to use a school level variable as a measure of the incidence or frequency of occurrence of each of the forms of illiteracy. The measure used was the proportion of all pupils in the school who were named by the rater(s) as having each of the four literacy problems defined in the literacy questionnaire. Pupils who were rated as having a problem with reading for general purposes were not counted again as having a problem with reading for further schooling; it was assumed that the former problem would include the latter. The same principle was applied in the case of writing for general purposes. The basic figures entering into calculations of the frequency of occurrence of each of the four literacy problems were, therefore, four overall school proportions.

Certain schools were excluded from the analysis. As indicated above, unless the ratings were made by a class teacher they were excluded. Furthermore, in some city and town schools (*n*:11), large enough to have more than one sixth class, not all of the sixth class teachers completed the questionnaire. Since we had no way of knowing whether the classes rated were typical of the school as a whole, it was again not possible to pool the proportions for these classes with those representing entire schools.*

Because of the widely differing degrees of representation in

*In schools where the pupils were rated by the principal or remedial teacher, a far smaller proportion of the pupils was considered to have the reading problem under discussion. The mean proportions in schools where only some of the classes were rated differ from those of other schools in their categories quite markedly and in different directions. These variations probably spring from differences in the characteristics of the particular classes rated, e.g., average or typical classes in some schools and a lower ability class in others; they justify our not including such schools in the overall means.

the sample of the population of schools in each category, it was necessary to weight the category means when obtaining the overall mean. The weight applied was computed by dividing the porportion in the sample of schools in that category whose responses met the criteria (all pupils rated by class teachers) and whose proprtions, therefore, were included in the category mean. Weights varied from 0.146 for town girls' schools which were over-represented in the sample as a whole to 2.372 for rural mixed schools which were under-represented.

Results

The mean proportions across schools of pupils judged as having each of the problems with literacy described in the questionnaire are reported in *Table 8.2*. Means are reported separately for each category of school. Overall means, both unweighted and weighted are given, along with the 95 per cent confidence intervals for the weighted means.

Table 8.2 *Mean Percentages of Pupils Reported as Having Each of Four Problems with Literacy*

School type	*Number of schools*	*Number of pupils*		*Literacy problem*			
		Range	*Total*	*Reading—general*	*Writing—general*	*Reading—schooling*	*Writing—schooling*
City Boys	12	14-145	935	4.3	4.8	4.8	1.3
City Girls	13	11-156	974	6.4	6.7	4.5	4.2
Town Boys	12	33-128	650	8.1	8.7	6.0	5.5
Town Girls	14	27-118	884	4.3	5.4	5.6	3.5
Rural Boys	8	7-25	131	5.2	5.4	5.6	4.7
Rural Girls	4	8-29	67	8.4	8.4	9.3	1.7
Rural Mixed	30	4-33	456	6.3	6.6	0	5.7
Unweighted means	93		4097	6.0	6.5	6.1	4.3
Weighted means (95% confidence interval)	93			6.2 (0.038-0.088	6.6 (0.042-0.090)	7.0 (0.054-0.086)	5.2 (0.036-0.068)

The figures indicate that we should expect about 6.2 per cent of the pupils in a randomly selected school in the country to be rated by their teachers as experiencing the degree of difficulty with reading described as "inability to cope with everyday demands." Because of sampling errors this figure may be as low as 3.8 per cent or as high as 8.6 per cent, but it is unlikely (only 5 chances in 100) that it falls outside this range. Mean percentages for schools grouped by location range from 4.3 per cent for city boys' schools and town girls' schools to 8.4 per cent for rural girls' schools.

The figures in the case of inability to cope with the demands for writing in society are a little higher than in the case of reading; 6.6 per cent (almost certainly not less than 4 per cent or more than 9 per cent) of sixth class pupils in a randomly selected school in the country would be expected to be judged by their teachers as being unable to cope with societal demands for writing if they were to end their schooling with their current year. The lowest percentage, 4.8, is reported for city boys' schools, and the highest, 8.7, for town boys' schools.

As far as reading and writing in the context of further schooling is concerned, for schools on the whole, 7 per cent is a realistic expectation of the number of sixth class pupils who, although they can read well enough to get on in general, would be judged to have problems with reading as a tool for further learning; 5.4 and 8.6 per cent are reasonable lower and upper bounds for this expectation, taking account of sampling errors. City and town schools are highly consistent in judging 4.5 to 6.0 per cent of their pupils as being unable to cope with the reading demands of further schooling. Rural schools vary widely, with boys' schools having the highest proportions of such pupils – an average of 9.3 per cent.

Somewhat lower proprotions of pupils are generally judged to be deficient specifically in the writing skills required for post-primary schooling than are judged to be so in the reading skills. On average, schools could be expected to have about 5.2 per cent (almost certainly not less than 3.6 or more than 6.8%) of their sixth class pupils judged by teachers to be lacking in the writing skills required for post-primary schooling, although they are judged to be able to write well enough to get on in ordinary daily life. City boys' schools and rural girls' schools report a low incidence of this problem, 1.3 and 1.7 per cent, respectively. The highest means, 5.5 and 5.7 per cent come from town boys' and rural mixed schools, respectively.

Correlates of Illiteracy

The focus of the second section of this investigation is on a comparison between pupils rated as having literacy problems and those not so rated in terms of standarised test performance and personal-social characteristics. For these comparisons, there is a change in the unit of analysis from the school to the individual pupil.

To compare the characteristics of pupils considered by teachers to have literacy problems, the mean value for pupils who were rated as having each of the four literacy problems was compared with the mean value for pupils not so rated on a number of variables. The variables on which comparisons were made were the pupil's age in months (on 15 October 1975), the pupil's raw score on the sub-tests of the Drumcondra English Tests Level III, the pupil's standard score on the Drumcondra Verbal Reasoning Test and the ratings of the pupil by the teacher on twelve personal-social characteristics. Average ratings were calculated for two subsets of these twelve characteristics; eight were regarded as constituting a school characteristics index and four as contributing to a general characteristics index.

In addition, information on two discrete personal-social variables was available. One was the occupational status of the pupil's father; the other was the type of post-primary school which was considered to be most suitable for pupils by their sixth class teacher. Pupils in each literacy problem area were categorised on the basis of these variables.

Finally, the extent to which reading and writing handicaps, at each of the levels described, were related to each other was determined by classifying and counting the pupils who had been rated as having the reading problem only, as having the writing problem only, and as having both problems.

Results

The results from the calculations of the means of age, test

scores, and personal-social ratings of pupils who were and were not identified as having each literacy problem are presented in *Table 8.3*. The numbers of cases involved in each comparison differ because test and rating information was not available for all pupils.

As far as age is concerned, children who have reading and writing difficulties are older than their classmates – by five to six months in the case of severe difficulties (i.e., for everyday purposes) and by about three months in the case of the less severe difficulties (i.e., for post-primary schooling). This age difference probably reflects a higher incidence of retention among the poorer readers and writers.

Not unexpectedly, markedly low mean attainment test scores were found among the pupils with reading and writing problems. While the mean score of the entire group of pupils was close to the standarisation mean (and so near the fiftieth percentile), pupils with difficulties in reading for everyday purposes had means around the eleventh to twelfth percentiles of the original distributions. Pupils with problems in writing for everyday purposes had slightly higher means on the attainment test scores (near the twelfth to fourteenth percentiles), while pupils with milder deficiencies in reading and writing scored near the eighteenth to twentieth percentiles.

On the Drumcondra Verbal Reasoning Test, pupils with severe reading and writing skill deficits had a standard score of 81 or 82; those with more moderate deficits had a standard score of 90 to 91.

On seven of the twelve personal-social ratings, pupils with the more serious reading and writing difficulties had mean scores of almost exactly 2 (fair) while their classmates' average ratings were about 3.5 (average to good); these traits were participation in class, attention and concentration, persistence in school work, keenness to get on, neatness in school work, working with limited supervision, and speech. Six of these characteristics were from the group considered school-related, and the seventh, speech, obviously has a higher cognitive component than the other three in the general characteristics category. For behaviour in class, attendance, personal appearance and dress, manners and politeness, and getting along with other children, the most seriously handicapped pupils averaged scores of 3 to 3.5 (average

Table 8.3 *Mean Test Scores and Personal–Social Characteristics Ratings of Pupils Rated as Having or Not Having Reading and Writing Difficulties*

Variable	*Number of pupils*	*Type and degree of difficulty*					
		Reading			*Writing*		
		Severe	*Moderate*	*None*	*Severe*	*Moderate*	*None*
	Total number in tested respondent schools	(218)	(217)	(3758)	(245)	(145)	(3803)
	Total number in pupil file	(196)	(199)	(3535)	(216)	(137)	(3577)
	Total number for age	(192)	(199)	(3438)	(213)	(137)	(3479)
Age		148.1	145.3	142.1	147.4	145.2	142.2
	Total number for attainment tests	(120)	(150)	(2180)	(145)	(105)	(2200)
English reading vocabulary		15.3	19.2	31.2	16.5	20.7	30.9
English reading comprehension		16.7	21.6	30.9	17.2	22.4	30.8
English reading total		31.8	41.0	62.2	33.7	43.1	61.9
English language		32.4	37.2	50.2	33.2	37.9	50.0
English spelling		27.8	30.8	38.9	28.4	31.4	38.8
	Total number for ability test	(163)	(178)	(3171)	(178)	(126)	(3208)
Verbal reasoning		81.4	90.1	106.3	81.9	91.0	106.1
	Total number for ratings	(145)	(165)	(2905)	(165)	(110)	(2940)
Participation in class		1.9	2.4	3.7	2.0	2.4	3.7
Behaviour in class		3.0	3.4	4.2	3.1	3.5	4.1
Attention, concentration		1.8	2.1	3.6	1.8	2.2	3.6
Persistence in school work		1.8	2.2	3.6	1.8	2.2	3.6
Keenness to get on		1.9	2.4	3.7	1.9	2.4	3.7
Neatness in school work		2.0	2.4	3.7	2.1	2.3	3.7
Working with limited supervision		1.9	2.2	3.6	1.9	2.3	3.6
Attendance		3.5	3.8	4.4	3.6	3.8	4.4
School characteristics average		2.2	2.6	3.8	2.3	2.6	3.8
Personal appearance, dress		3.2	3.7	4.3	3.3	3.8	4.3
Speech		2.0	2.5	3.7	2.1	2.4	3.7
Manners, politeness		3.2	3.5	4.3	3.4	3.6	4.2
Getting along with other children		3.1	3.6	4.1	3.2	3.6	4.0
General characteristics average		2.9	3.3	4.1	3.0	3.3	4.1

or better), but their classmates without comparable reading and writing problems scored 4 (good) or slightly higher on these traits.

An almost identical pattern occurred for the less severely deficient readers and writers. In these cases, however, the means for the pupil behaviours were somewhat higher than in the case of the more handicapped readers and writers though still not as high as for pupils who were not judged to have literacy problems.

The relationship between the incidence of reading and writing skill deficiencies and the occupational status of fathers is shown in *Table 8.4.* The number of pupils who had fathers in professional/managerial or white collar jobs was low among the handicapped readers and writers. Children of skilled and unskilled workers, on the other hand, appeared in each of the problem type categories with roughly the same frequency as they do in the rest of the pupil sample, with a few exceptions. There was a slightly higher incidence of moderate reading disability among children of skilled workers and unskilled workers, of severe writing disability among children of unskilled workers,

Table 8.4 *Occupational Status of Fathers of Pupils Rated as Having or Not Having Reading and Writing Difficulties*

	Type and degree of difficulty					
	Reading			*Writing*		
Occupational Status	*Severe* (148)	*Moderate* (169)	*None* (3025)	*Severe* (169)	*Moderate* (112)	*None* (3061)
Professional/managerial	4.7	1.8	8.6	3.6	2.7	8.5
Middle-class/white collar	4.1	8.3	18.9	4.1	8.9	18.8
Skilled worker	23.6	29.6	25.8	24.9	24.1	26.0
Unskilled worker	20.3	22.5	18.8	23.7	19.6	18.8
Farmer, ≥ 50 acres	4.1	1.8	3.7	3.0	3.6	3.7
Farmer, < 50 acres	4.7	10.7	4.6	2.4	10.7	4.8
Unemployed, invalid unreported, unclassifable	34.5	21.9	17.5	33.7	26.8	17.3
Dead	4.1	3.6	2.1	4.7	3.6	2.1

and of moderate reading and writing disabilities among the children of farmers of small acreage. There was, on the other hand, a slightly lower incidence of moderate writing problems among children of farmers of large acreage. The most startling incidence of handicap was reported for children of fathers who were unemployed, invalided or dead or whose occupations were not reported or not reported accurately by the class teachers; far higher percentages of these pupils had severe and moderate handicaps in reading and in writing than their membership in the total group would have led one to expect.

Sixth class teachers' judgements about the most suitable kind of post-primary school for pupils with the varying degrees of reading and writing disability and with no disability are shown in *Table 8.5.* While, in general, teachers recommended that about 50 per cent of pupils should go to secondary school, 25 per cent to vocational school and 20 per cent to comprehensive school, few pupils (4.2 to 9 per cent) who were perceived as having reading and writing problems were regarded as suitable for secondary schooling. A large number of such pupils (57 to 62 per cent) were, however, regarded as suitable for vocational schooling. For a relatively large number of pupils with literacy problems (16 to 25 per cent) teachers were unsure what kind of post-primary school would be most suitable. It was only in the case of comprehensive schools, that teachers' recommendations

Table 8.5 *Teacher Judgement of Most Suitable Type of Post-primary School for Pupils Rated as Having or Not having Reading and Writing Difficulties*

	Type and degree of difficulty					
	Reading			*Writing*		
Type of post-primary school	*Severe* (144)	*Moderate* (158)	*None* (2894)	*Severe* (161)	*Moderate* (100)	*None* (2935)
Secondary	4.2	7.0	52.2	5.0	9.0	51.5
Vocational	60.4	59.5	24.3	61.5	57.0	24.8
Comprehensive	17.4	13.3	18.4	18.0	9.0	18.4
Too soon to tell	18.1	20.3	5.0	15.5	25.0	5.2

did not take reading disability into account, though even here there was a tendency not to recommend such a school for pupils who were perceived as likely to have difficulties in post-primary schools.

The final relationship to be considered is that between having reading difficulty and having writing difficulty at each of the two levels, everyday use and further schooling. Of the pupils rated as having a reading handicap which would leave them unable to cope with the demands of everyday life, 65 per cent were also reported to have a writing handicap; 22 per cent were judged to have only a writing handicap and 13 per cent to have only a reading handicap. Among pupils judged to have a reading or a writing handicap in coping with the demands of post-primary schooling, 52 per cent were reported to have both handicaps, 38 per cent to have only the reading handicap, and 9 per cent to have only the writing handicap.

Discussion

Our findings indicate that the average percentage of sixth standard pupils per school rated by teachers as being unable to cope with the reading demands of everyday life is about 6 per cent. A further 7 per cent are regarded as unable to read well enough to cope with the demands of post-primary school. The corresponding figures for writing are 6.6 and 5.2 per cent. If we assume that pupils who are unable to cope with everyday demands would also be unable to cope with the demands of post-primary school and if all pupils in sixth classes transfer to such schools, then we would expect that teachers in the typical primary school consider 13.2 per cent of pupils going to post-primary school as unable to cope with the reading demands of the school and 11.8 per cent as unable to cope with the writing demands of the school. The problem, obviously, is not an insignificant one for post-primary schools.

As one would expect, there is considerable overlap between pupils with reading and writing disabilities. Fifty-nine per cent of the pupils with disabilities have them in both the areas of reading and writing; 25 per cent have only a reading problem while 16 per cent have a writing problem only.

Our data on the characteristics of poor readers and writers

can hardly be regarded as very surprising. Such children tend to be older than other children in their class, while their verbal reasoning scores and their scores on standardised tests of English attainment are considerably below average. On ratings of their personal-social characteristics by teachers, pupils with learning disabilities score considerably lower than other children; that is particularly so for characteristics that are closely related to scholastic performance, such as concentration, persistence and use of language. It is worth noting that for social characteristics, such as manners, class behaviour and getting on with other children, their ratings, while still lower than those for other children, are closer than in the case of more school-related characteristics. Problems associated with literacy, as has been found in many other studies[6] are related to social class membership. These findings on correlates of the problem of literacy serve to underline its complexity. Obviously, the problem does not occur in isolation, but resides in a complex network of personal and social factors.

In conclusion, our findings that teachers perceive problems of literacy to the extent documented in this study confirm much of the concern that has been expressed about these problems from a variety of sources in recent years. Our data indicate something of the complexity of the problem though they do little to unravel it. While it is normal, and sometimes platitudinous, to end research reports by indicating the need for further research, the seriousness of the problem under consideration, together with our present level of knowledge about it, indicates that in this case, failure to make such a recommendation would be a serious omission. Too many teachers have struggled with the problem for too long, and there is no evidence that simplistic solutions will do much to solve it in the future. Despite the best efforts of a great many teachers, the problem remains and is likely to remain in the future. It seems clear that until we achieve a greater understanding of problems related to learning to read – which understanding ultimately depends on the availability of more research evidence – a large number of teachers and pupils are condemned to continue with their present inadequate efforts to cope with such problems.

References

1. Resnick, D.P., and Resnick, L.B. The nature of literacy: An historical exploration. *Harvard Educational Review*, 1977, *47* 370-385.
2. Great Britain: Ministry of Education. *Reading ability*. London: HMSO, 1950.
3. Nafziger, D.H., Thompson, R.B., Hiscox, M.D., and Owen, T.R. *Tests of functional adult literacy: An evaluation of currently available instruments.* Portland, Oregon: Northwest Regional Educational Laboratory, 1976.
4. Educational Research Centre. *Drumcondra Verbal Reasoning Test.* Dublin: Educational Research Centre, St Patrick's College, 1968.
5. Educational Research Centre. *Drumcondra Attainment Tests, Level III, Form A. Manual.* Dublin: Educational Research Centre, St Patrick's College, 1977.
6. Seitz, V. *Social class and ethnic group differences in learning to read.* Newark, Delaware: International Reading Association, 1977.

III. STUDIES OF THE READING PROCESS

9. *An Experimental Investigation of the Psycholinguistic Model of the Reading Process*

*Gerard M. Ryan, Psychology Department, University College, Dublin**

Attempts to develop theoretical models of the psychological operations involved in reading for meaning are now frequent among reading researchers. Psycholinguistic models of the reading process suggest that skilled reading is not a precise visual process but is rather a constructive language-related process. These models emphasise the reader's utilisation of orthographic, graphophonic, syntactic and semantic sources of redundant information during continuous oral (or silent) reading. Readers' ability to dynamically utilise these redundant sources of information is believed to facilitate their extraction of meaning from print, by means of highly selective perceptual sampling of available information.

The present study investigated some implications of Goodman's[1, 2] psycholinguistic model of the reading process. This model emphasises the importance of readers' hypothesis-formation and perceptual sampling strategies in the process of continuous oral (or silent) reading of semantically related sentential material. Arising out of previous research in both skilled and beginning reading processes, a number of hypotheses were formulated, concerning the interactions which may occur between readers' usage of graphic and contextual information during continuous oral reading.

*The author wishes to express his appreciation to Rev. Professor E.F. O'Doherty, Dr. Anne McKenna and Professor T.D. Swan for their invaluable assistance during the completion of this research project.

Research Methodology

Twenty slow and twenty average 12-year old, sixth-grade readers served as subjects for the experiment. Selected subjects were matched in terms of socio-economic status, chronological age (i.e. 11.5 to 12.5 years), sex (10 boys and 10 girls in each group), grade level at primary school, and non-verbal reasoning performance (as measured by Raven's Standard Progressive Matrices, Sets A, B, C, D and E). Slow and average readers were then differentiated in terms of their respective performances on two tests of reading comprehension, N.F.E.R. Reading Tests S2 and SRB. Selection of subjects for the experimental stages of the investigation involved the administration of the aforementioned psychological tests to an original sample of 165 sixth grade children, with an age range of 11.5 to 12.5 years.

The experimental design employed was a 2 x 3 x 3 repeated-measures factorial design, with repeated measures on two treatment factors. Subjects were required to read three different 120-word prose passages under stimulus conditions involving varying amounts of graphic and prior contextual information. The oral reading errors or "miscues" generated by the children in processing the graphic displays were analysed in terms of both quantitative and qualitative taxonomic criteria developed by Goodman and Burke.[3] The quantitative analysis involved the classification of readers' miscues in terms of five major response categories, viz., substitutions, omissions, insertions, reversals and repetitions of an item or a group of items. The qualitative analysis involved the classification of oral reading errors in terms of six major response categories, namely, graphic similarity; grammatical function; correction; syntactic acceptability; semantic acceptability; and meaning change. Miscue analysis of the utilisation of these qualitative response categories enabled the researcher to determine the extent of the reader's relative dependence upon graphical and contextual information for word-recognition during continuous oral reading.

Results

Results indicate that Goodman's psycholinguistic model does

not provide an entirely valid characterisation of the information-processing strategies of slower as compared with average 12-year-old readers. The generalisability of Goodman's model of the successful reader is seriously questioned in a number of important respects. Results indicate that the processing strategies of slower and average readers manifest differences which are not predicted by a generalised model of the psychological operations involved in reading for meaning.

1 Results concerning readers' usage of graphic information suggest that Goodman's psycholinguistic model overestimates the extent to which younger readers' usage of contextual cues may facilitate their adoption of a perceptual strategy for selectively sampling the graphic display. While slower readers were considerably more dependent upon the use of graphemic cues for word-recognition than average readers, average readers utilised selective perceptual sampling strategies to a relatively stable extent only under conditions involving levels of syntactic redundancy and semantic context that are presumably far greater than those operative in more normal reading tasks.
2 Results concerning readers' usage of grammatical information indicate that both slower and average readers actively transform the grammatical structure of the text, during continuous oral reading. Although average readers generate more miscues that retain the grammatical function of the expected "correct" response than slower readers, each group of readers also engaged in active transformations of available grammatical cues. These results indicate that readers' processing of grammatical information is not as dependent upon their simultaneous usage of prior contextual cues as Goodman's model has suggested. It is suggested that this particular taxonomic category does not provide an entirely valid index of readers' processing of grammatical information since readers actively transformed the grammatical structure of textual words, whereas Goodman's model proposes that skilled reading processes involve the construction of miscue responses that retain the grammatical features of the graphic display. Both slower and average readers attempt to integrate word meanings into higher-order semantic structures and

these integrative processes do not necessarily involve the reader's precise processing of the grammatical information encoded in textual words. The qualitative analysis of readers' usage of grammatical information provided in Goodman and Burke's[3] Reading Miscue Inventory does not give adequate attention to the existence of such constructive strategies in readers' processing of semantically related sentential material.

3 Results concerning readers' correction strategies suggest that Goodman's psycholinguistic model does not provide an adequate specification of which processing stage (or stages) may be facilitated through readers' usage of semantic and syntactic information. It is suggested that Goodman's psycholinguistic model does not give adequate attention to the possibility that slower and average readers' utilisation of prior contextual information may exert significant psychological effects during rather different stages of their respective information processing strategies.

4 Results concerning readers' usage of syntactic information are not entirely consistent with Goodman's model, in so far as they indicate that increasing degrees of contextual constraint exerted considerably different effects upon slower as compared with average readers' processing of syntactic information and were predominantly manifested in their construction of partially acceptable syntactic structures, whereas improvements which occurred in average readers' processing of syntactic cues were predominantly manifested in their construction of totally acceptable syntactic structures.

In conjunction with the results concerning readers' processing of semantic information and readers' comprehension strategies, these differences between slower and average readers' usage of further graphic and contextual information are interpreted in terms of a constructive model of sentence comprehension which emphasises the importance for comprehension of the semantic context active during sentence processing. It is suggested that average readers' utilisation of prior contextual information facilitates their construction of a "holistic" semantic representation of the information expressed by consecutive, semantically related sentences, whereas slower readers' utilisation of prior contextual cues facilitates their comprehension of the information expressed in single sentences. The results also indicate that not all categories of Goodman's Taxonomy of Oral Reading Miscues provide equally valid information concerning readers' processing strategies. A fruitful area of further research in miscue analysis may reside in the specification of those features of Goodman's complex taxonomy which yield more valid information about readers' usage of prior contextual information during continuous oral reading. Finally, some attention is devoted to the statistical and theoretical problem involved in the usage of multiple comparison procedures following the analysis of variance.

References

1. Goodman, K.S. Reading: A psycholinguistic guessing game. *Journal of the Reading Specialist*, 1967, 4, 126-35.
2. Goodman, K.S. Analysis of oral reading miscues: Applied psycholinguistics. *Reading Research Quarterly*, 1969, 5, 9 - 30.
3. Goodman, Y.M. and Burke, C.L. *Reading Miscue Inventory: Procedure for Diagnosis and evaluation*. New York: MacMillan, 1972.
4. Ryan, G.M. *An Experimental Investigation of the Psycholinguistic Model of the Reading Process*. Unpublished Master's Thesis, Department of Logic and Psychology, University College, Belfield, Dublin 4. June, 1978.

10. A Study of Reading Errors Using Goodman's Miscue Analysis and Cloze Procedure

Seán N. Farren, Education Centre, The New University of Ulster

Introduction

Error analysis is a well established approach in the study of human behaviour. Weber has reviewed its application to reading research and argues that two separate schools can be identified.[1] One, she claims is concerned with using error analysis as a basis for constructing remedial programmes while the second is more interested in the insights offered through error analysis into basic reading strategies.

One of the most notable voices in the second school in recent years has been that of Kenneth Goodman who has developed the "psycholinguistic guessing game" concept of reading. This concept stresses the reader's active role in interpreting a set of highly structured cues of different kinds, graphic, phonemic, syntactic and semantic. These sets of cues are made to interact by the reader on the basis of his existing knowledge of them. From this interaction results an understanding of the text's message which matches to a greater or lesser extent that of its author and those of other readers.

Differences as to an author's meaning which may arise between readers can be accounted for in terms of their differential use and interpretation of this set of cues. Some of this differential use of cues is, claims Goodman, manifested in the errors, or miscues as he prefers to term them, which readers make. In other words, whenever a reader incorrectly identifies the words of a text an error, or miscue, has been made. Since, according to Goodman, these errors are not normally causal but rather are the outcome of the particular reader's attempt to interpret the available cues, an examination of them can provide insights into the reading strategies being used.

A considerable body of research has developed on the basis of Goodman's thesis. One particular focus in this research has been readers' ability to exploit their knowledge of the grammatical rules of language. Goodman has demonstrated how readers can anticipate and predict what may follow in a text on the basis of this knowledge, and also their ability to correct spontaneously errors which arise when anticipations turn out to be inaccurate.[2]

Weber in a study of reading errors made by first grade pupils has shown the extent to which these errors respected the grammatical structure of the sentences in which they occurred.[3] Only about 10 per cent of the sentences were rendered completely ungrammatical by these errors. The other 90 per cent were either completely grammatical (60 per cent), or grammatical up to and including the error.

On the basis of such findings it would appear that pupils, even at this early stage of formal reading instruction, are capable of responding appropriately to many, if not most, of the grammatical cues in their texts.

Following these and other studies, a general recommendation to make special use of context as a means of exploiting readers' grammatical knowledge as an aid to correct reading has been appearing in the literature on reading instruction.[4] Biemiller, however, has challenged the extent to which such a recommendation should be heeded.[5] He argues that it is the graphic cues which present the main problem to initial readers since it is precisely such cues which are least familiar to them. Knowledge of grammatical cues is generally already well established through mastery of oral language, and while it may be an effective tactic in certain instances to exploit this knowledge, Biemiller claims that any neglect of graphic cues ignores the principal learning task and may make for future problems. He states that "the child's early use of contextual information does not appear to greatly facilitate progress in acquiring reading skill." Instead, he recommends that "teachers do a considerable proportion of early reading training in situations providing no context at all in order to compel children to use graphic information as much as possible."

There is, therefore, some debate arising out of recent error studies as to the implications they might hold for reading instruction. The recommendations instanced above, while not mutually exclusive, do tend to suggest contrasting bases for the initial teaching of reading and perhaps for helping readers whose rate of progress is below average.

It is with a group of the latter kind that the present study is concerned. Error analysis literature has little to say about such readers. Weber refers to a number of studies, Swanson,[6] Fairbanks,[7] Bennett[8] and Malmquist.[9] Bennett concludes that poor readers evidence a tendency to give a response associated with the stimulus before it is fully perceived, suggesting inadequately developed powers of graphic analysis. Weber[3] and Fairbanks note a tendency for such readers to correct errors less than good readers do, perhaps an indication of poor response to the semantic cues of a text.[3,7]

Sample and Procedures

The present study examines errors made by 11 boys all aged between 12 and 14 whose reading abilities ranged from 7 to 9 on the Schonell (W.R.T.) scale. Most of them had been receiving remedial reading instruction since primary school. In their secondary school, remedial classes were conducted on a withdrawal basis of approximately four forty-minute periods per week. The author worked with the boys in question over a term spent as a member of the remedial team. In order to assess whether differences might exist between error patterns in silent and oral reading it was decided to sample pupils' reading in both modes.

Oral reading was sampled in the traditional way. Pupils were allowed to glance briefly over the texts before reading them aloud to a tape recorder. Copies of these texts were later annotated to reflect any errors made. Cloze procedure was used to sample silent reading. Following a short deletion-free introduction of 2 to 3 sentences, texts contained deletions at every tenth word. It is obvious that cloze has severe limitations as a means of sampling errors since it is only possible to obtain such evidence at the choice points predetermined by the deletions. However, any other means of sampling errors in silent reading are likely to be even more indirect.

The texts chosen for both kinds of reading were taken from the 'Reading Routes' laboratory[10] and were at reading levels between 7.5 and 9.

Results and Discussion

Errors in oral reading were defined as any mispronunciation, omission, insertion or substitution of words. Any obvious disregard of punctuation was also noted. Repetitions, however, while noted were not counted as errors, although some studies would so classify them. A record was made of all errors spontaneously corrected by the pupils. In cloze readings, errors were defined as any response differing in any way from the deleted word. A total of 284 errors were noted in the oral readings and 495 in the cloze. Goodman's "Taxonomy of Cues and Miscues in Reading"[11] was used as a guide to the analysis. Within this taxonomy Goodman first categorises errors according to their linguistic nature, i.e. graphic, semantic, syntactic etc., and secondly scales them in terms of their proximity to the expected response. The present study confines the linguistic analysis only to the more general categories and avoids the very discreet sub-classifications offered by Goodman.

The scaling system proposed is a nine or ten point one depending on the kind of cue. For example, from the data collected, "says" was substituted for "said." This error was ranked at 4 on the graphic scale since it contained two letters similar to its "expected response" out of a possible four. At the syntactic level it was ranked at 6 since the only change involved was one of tense, while at the semantic level it was also ranked 6 there being, apparently, only a slight change of meaning as a result.

Using Goodman's taxonomy and its scaling principle the resulted displayed in Tables 10.1 and 10.2 were obtained. These tables indicate the number of errors at graphic, syntactic and semantic levels according to their degree of proximity to the expected response. Mean values for the errors are also indicated.

In both sets of data one is immediately struck by the high number of errors concentrated round the extremes of the scale. At each of the three levels in both the oral and the cloze readings, errors tended to be either quite proximate or not very proximate to their expected response.

When examined more closely, the overall picture presents a number of interesting and similar patterns across both sets of data. These patterns are most readily seen in the two bar graphs (*Fig. 10.1*).

Here the errors are shown as divided into three groups at each level, those least proximate to their expected response (scale points 0, 1, 2), those at the centre of the scale (points 3, 4, 5) and those most proximate to their expected response (points 6, 7, 8, 9). In the oral reading results a similar pattern of error distribution across the scale can be seen for both the graphic and the syntactic levels, i.e. a high number of errors at both extremes, fewer at the centre, but with the highest number appearing in the most proximate group. This pattern is, however, virtually reversed at the semantic level where the highest number of errors were judged to be of very low or zero proximity to their expected responses. The cloze reading results present a very similar distribution pattern at both the syntactic and semantic level.

A first conclusion therefore might be that both sets of errors would appear to be having similar effects in the sense that they suggest readings tending to be of the same degree of proximity to the original. Apart from anything else, this could be taken as confirming the claim that oral and silent reading are parallel processes.

More pertinent for assessing pedagogic implications is an examination of the results at the syntactic level and a comparison between what seems to be happening at that level with what is revealed about the other two. The syntactic level is chosen as a key level for discussion because, as indicated above, it has been the level to have received a great deal of attention in previous studies.

Results at the syntactic level suggest that about 60 per cent of the errors are highly proximate to their expected response. However, since the effect of the remaining 40 per cent would not necessarily be the creation of grammatically unacceptable

Fig. 10.1 Percentage distribution of errors according to proximity values.

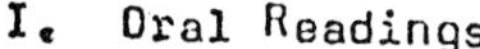

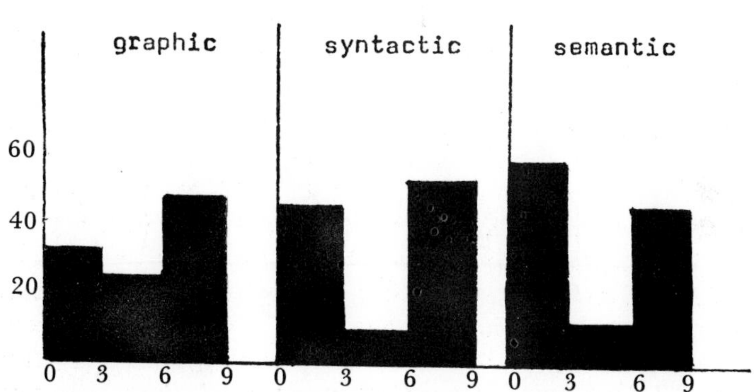

2. Silent Readings (cloze)

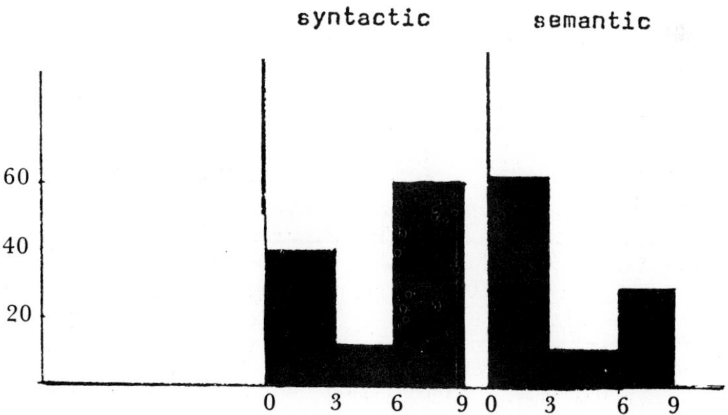

sentences, it was decided to examine all sentences containing errors to see to what extent they might be still grammatical. Grammatically correct sentences would indicate that readers were responding appropriately to grammatical cues.

Table 10.1 *Oral Reading Errors – Proximity Values (n. 284)*

Degrees of proximity	0	1	2	3	4	5	6	7	8	9	*Mean*
Graphic	73	8	10	27	34	6	50	20	56	0	4.1
Syntactic	116	1	0	4	5	4	38	11	105		4.2
Semantic	159	0	1	1	15	0	26	22	48		3.0

Table 10.2 *Silent (Cloze) Reading Errors – Proximity Values (n. 495)*

Degrees of proximity	0	1	2	3	4	5	6	7	8	9	*Mean*
Syntactic	169	15	5	0	4	1	33	47	221		4.7
Semantic	210	0	112	0	36	0	73	15	44	4	2.6

Table 10.3 *Grammatical effect of errors on sentences*

	Grammatical to end	*Grammatical to error, ungramm. to end*	*Ungrammatical*
Farren (oral)	60 (172)*	28 (79)	12 (34)
Farren (silent)	59 (292)	17.2 (85)	22.2 (110)
Weber (oral)	55.9 (52)	36.6 (34)	7.6 (7)

*bracketed figures represent actual number of errors

Weber's approach was followed.[3] She proposes 3 possible kinds of sentence consequent to an error (a) sentences grammatical to the end, (b) sentences grammatical up to and including the error, (c) completely ungrammatical sentences. *Table 10.3* summarises the findings of this analysis and offers comparison with Weber's results for her low ability readers. In this latter respect similar results would appear to exist across both studies. Approximately 60 per cent of errors do not affect the grammaticality of sentences. A further 28 per cent in the case of oral reading and 17 per cent in cloze lead to semi-grammatical sentences. In Weber's study this second figure is somewhat higher at almost 37 per cent. Overall, however, the point can be stressed that in more than three-quarters of the errors readers were responding appropriately to grammatical cues, to a greater or lesser extent. If this conclusion is correct it would indicate that, in the case of such low ability readers as those involved in this study, response strategies to grammatical cues are good, just as they were shown to be in the case of low ability readers at first grade in Weber's study.

If grammatical cues are being appropriately responded to for the most part, can the same be said of cues at each of the other two levels?

Consideration of errors at the graphic level suggests a similar, but more even distribution, across the scale (*Table 10.1*).

At this level also the most proximate group is the largest group of the three, but at 44 per cent it contains less than half of the errors. It would appear, therefore, that a higher degree of miscueing was taking place at this level. However, following the positive approach adopted in analysing the errors from a syntactic perspective an examination was made to determine in what ways errors retained similarity to their expected responses in graphic terms.

Table 10.4 *Source of error in graphemic terms*

Initial Grapheme	*Medial Grapheme*	*Final Grapheme*	*No Resemblance*
9 (25)*	21 (59)	46 (132)	23 (68)

*bracketed figures represent actual number of errors

Results (*Table 12.5*) indicate that 76 per cent of errors retained some graphic element of the expected response while the rest bore no resemblance at all to it. Is this evidence enough to suggest poor word attack skills in these readers? A closer examination of the 76 per cent retaining some similarity may help answer this question. This figure consists of the 9 per cent which reflect miscueing on the initial part of a word, e.g. "another" substituted for "other", "there" for "where" and "dig" for "big" etc. Twenty-one per cent contain a miscue on the medial section, or the medial and final sections, e.g. "last" for "least", "the" for "this" etc. Forty-six per cent reflect miscues on the final letters only, e.g. "with" for "witch", "pleased" for "pleasant" and a very large number where a plural form is substituted for a singular, and vice versa.

No clear evidence emerges from this data as to what kinds of graphemes, or graphemic combinations, might be causing particular difficulty. Indeed many of the words which are miscued are correctly responded to in other sentences thus making it even more difficult to detect any general pattern of word attack problems. What does seem to emerge, however, is some weakness in responding to graphic cues in context, i.e. what Bennett summarises as a tendency to give a response associated with the stimulus before it is fully perceived.[8] This is a tendency which may be influenced by the reader's more developed response strategies to grammatical cues. Of the 23 per cent of errors bearing no graphic resemblance to their expected response, some 60 per cent were grammatically acceptable substitutes, thus suggesting that grammatically acceptable miscues may distract from graphic cues. There is further evidence of this in the spontaneously corrected errors. Only 2 per cent of grammatically acceptable miscues were self-corrected in contrast to 17 per cent in the case of those creating ungrammatical sentences. These readers, therefore, would appear to be quite satisfied if they produce grammatically acceptable sentences whatever about graphic and semantic acceptability.

At the semantic level, errors judged in terms of their dictionary proximity to the expected response, tended to fall more into the lower of the three groups. It is a very pronounced tendency in both sets of data and although the final effect was not tested through any kind of comprehension test there would appear to be a general weakness in responding to meaning. The low level of self-correction already referred to could be further evidence of this.

Conclusions

Results of this study of reading errors made by eleven boys of poor reading ability at secondary level indicate a number of notable tendencies.

It is suggested that while such readers may appropriately exploit their ability to respond to grammatical cues they would appear to have poorly established strategies for responding to the graphic cues of words in a text. In addition a general weakness in responding to semantic cues was noted.

Further research is required before precise implications can be drawn from the study. A general implication suggested is that caution can be advised in encouraging pupils to use contextual cues where the ability to respond to graphic cues seems to be weak. This is in line with Biemiller's recommendations for the initial stages of reading instruction. Exercises which focus attention particularly on the post-initial parts of words would appear to be especially called for. These should not deal only with the words as isolated elements, but should contextualise them in a variety of ways and do so to provide opportunities for reading them in a variety of texts.

References and Bibliography

1. Weber, R.M. The study of oral reading errors: a survey of the literature. *Reading Research Quarterly*, 1968, 4, 96-119.
2. Goodman, K.S. A linguistic study of cues and miscues in reading. *Elementary English,* 1965, 42, 639-43.
   Goodman, K.S. Reading: a psycholinguistic guessing game. *Journal of the Reading Specialist*, 1967, 259-71.
3. Weber, R.M. First-graders use of grammatical context in reading. In H. Levin and J.P. Williams, *Basic Studies on reading,* New York, N.Y.; Random House. 1970, 147-163.
4. Chall, J. *Learning to Read: the great debate*, New York, N.Y.; McGraw-Hill, 1967.
5. Biemiller, A.J. The development and use of graphic and contextual

information as children learn to read. *Reading Research Quarterly*, 4, 1, 1970, 75-96.

6. Swanson, D.E. Common elements in silent and oral reading. *Psychological Monographs*, 1937, 48 (215), 36-60.
7. Fairbanks, G. The relation between eye-movements and voice in the oral reading of good and poor silent readers. *Psychological Monographs*, 1937, 48 (215), 78-107.
8. Bennett, A. An analysis of errors in word recognition made by retarded readers. *Journal of Educational Psychology*, 1942, 33, 25-38.
9. Malmquist, E. Factors related to reading disabilities in the first grade of the elementary school. Stockholm: Almquist and Wiksell, 1958.
10. Leedham, J. *Reading Routes*; London: Longman Group Ltd., 1973.
11. Goodman, K.S. Analysis of oral reading miscues: applied psycholinguistics. *Reading Research Quarterly*, 1969, V/1, 9-30.
12. Goodman, Y. A psycholinguistic description of oral reading phenomena in selected young beginning readers. Unpublished doctoral dissertation, Wayne State University, 1967.
13. Open University, *Reading purposes, comprehension and the use of context.* Units 3 and 4 of the Reading Development Course, Milton Keynes: The Open University Press, 1973.

11. Sentence Length and Sentence Complexity

Anne McKenna, Department of Psychology, University College, Dublin

Recent models of the reading process favour a multiskill approach with processing at the graphological, orthographic, lexical, syntactic and semantic levels. Whether such processes take place serially or in parallel is a question for future model makers but what is no longer in doubt is the complexity and variety of skills necessary at all stages. It has been strongly argued however that the relative proportions of contributory skills varies with the stage of proficiency, and a number of authors have argued for a two-model explanation, one for the aquisition process, the other for the skilled reading process.

Thus models such as in *Fig. 11.1a*, would indicate that the skills of sound-symbol relationship and visual discrimination are, in that order, more important initially, with language structure skills less so. In progressing from beginning reading to skilled reading, these proportions change, visual discrimination being of minimal importance with the proficient reader, and language skills or structures pre-eminent.

However if we think, not in terms of the child's difficulties, but rather of his competencies, the graphic representation would look quite different (*Fig. 11.1b*). Since the child of five or six years brings to the written page a well-formed and rehearsed language structure, such a structure would be his greatest competency, with visual discrimination coming next as a partially developed system, and letter-sound relationship, in which the child is a mere fledgling, last of all. Such well-formed language might then be seen as his main strength and chief support in

Fig. 11.1 (a) Relative dependencies at beginning and proficient stages of reading. (b) Relative competencies at beginning and proficient stages of reading. A = sound-symbol relationship, B = visual discrimination, C = language structures.

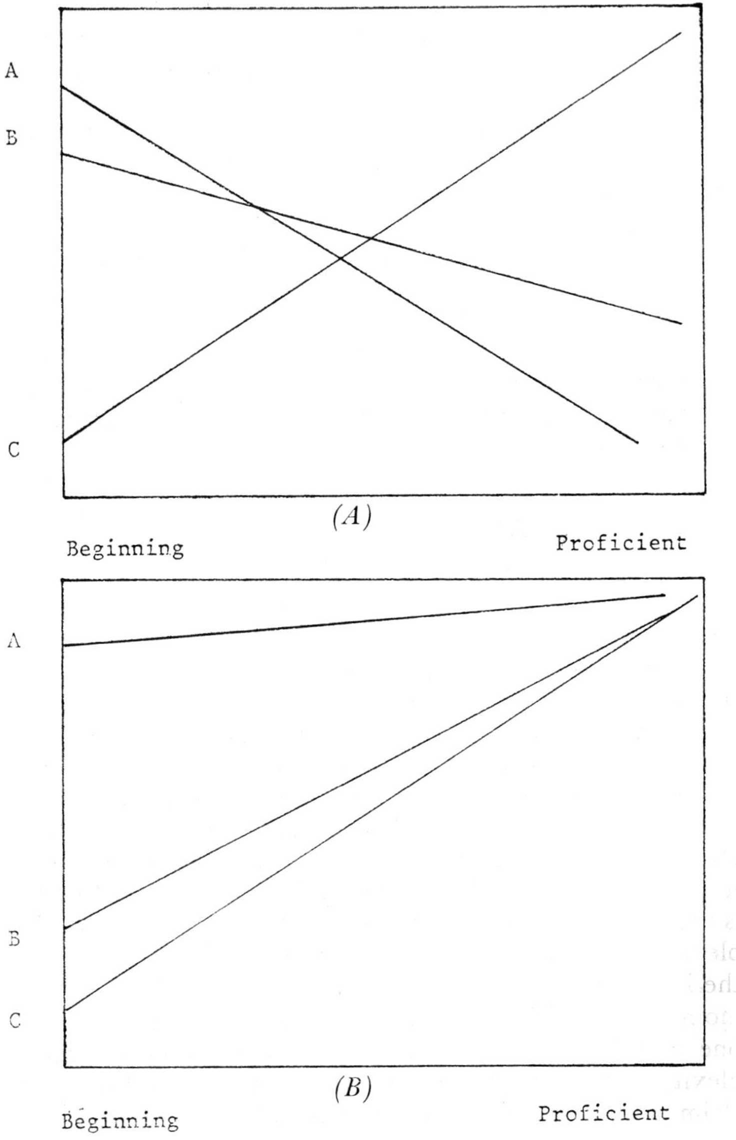

breaking the new code and starting to read. Reading being the mapping of speech onto paper in a highly abstract and schematic fashion, the underlying structure of speech which it represents must be seen as guiding the apprentice reader in his search and use of language regularities, and in his meaningful chunking of material. However this can only come about in the measure in which there is a match between the child's existing speech patterns and the written words in front of him. This seems an obvious thing to say, but our awareness and sensitivity to the need for enriching the child's language experience, of bringing it up to some hypothetical beginner-reader level, might deflect our interest from the reverse, but equally important process, namely that of bringing the language of reading material down to the child's level. The problem of matching for social class content has long been recognised, but the problem of matching for developmentally adequate patterns of speech has scarcely begun, for the very good reason that this has had to wait for the gathering of naturalistic data on which to base such patterns.

Matching Material to Child

What then is the child's state of development of spoken language when we present him with the task of moving to the secondary symbolic process of reading? Given that it should match his spoken language at least in the very first approaches to reading, how can we avoid a mismatch? Such a search will include considerations of appropriate vocabulary, phonic complexity, cognitive structures underlying semantics, and available syntactic structures. For such a task there is a growing body of knowledge about the development of meaning and grammar. Furthermore it would look as if this is relatively invariant for all children and is primarily determined by the semantic and grammatical complexity of constructions rather than frequency of occurrence in the language of adults surrounding the child.[1] However for the moment I would like to take up the claim of one writer, that one of the most effective methods of ordering sentence complexity in the initial stages, is that of sentence length.[1] Such a claim is an attractive one, because of its simplicity, and its applicability as a rule of thumb measure. It is not of course being claimed that each word adds another bead to the string, as in repeating a string of digits, nor that the difficulty lies merely in longer and therefore more difficult memory tasks. More important than constraints of memory storage are those of grammar and meaning.

Brown has set out a tentative plan of descriptive norms based on the analysis of eighteen children and this is in broad agreement with evidence from other more linguistically based studies.[2] He posits some thirty-three steps of cumulative complexity, which progress in conjunction with sentence length or more accurately utterance length. *Fig. 11.2* sets out the basic semantic and syntactic categories, in order of complexity, by mean length of utterance (M.L.U.).

Fig. 11.2

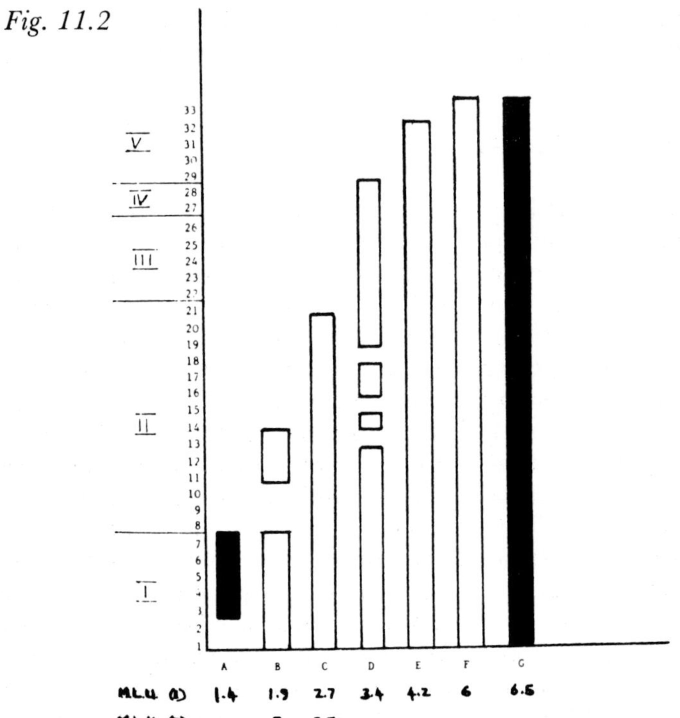

The vertical line represents cumulative ordering of the basic semantic and syntactic categories of the English language with the horizontal axis giving mean length of utterance, each child being represented by a letter of the alphabet and a bar. It should be noted that although the children are ordered by mean length of utterance, this does not correspond to age, which is an unsatisfactory longitudinal control in the language acquisition process. M.L.U. is measured in this case by calculation of morphemes, but since there are many linguistic objections to this measure, M.L.U. by word-count is also given – probably a less pretentious although less accurate measure. The graph bears out the finding of Brown, that the longer the sentence the more complex it is, at least up to the stage of acquisition of a four-morpheme utterance. It would also tend to confirm his findings that after this stage has been reached, sentence length ceases to be a measure of complexity. However, bearing in mind certain reservations, one might say that the shorter the sentence the simpler is the processing task – a finding which must have some relevance to the chunking of written material and to development of eye-voice span. The reservations, however, have to be borne in mind because the child himself is not writing his own reading material although such a method can now be seen as the logical outcome of psycholinguistic findings. But the adult might unwittingly produce a short complex sentence. Fortunately, however, with an order scale of language complexity to hand, we can now look forward to the possibility of a double ordering on the factors of both length and complexity simultaneously.

The common-sense assumption that what comes earliest must be easiest is backed up by the findings of investigations of the meaningfulness of vocabulary items. Such studies indicate that early acquired words are more important in producing the effects of frequency (imagery, meaningfulness and familiarity) than later acquisitions.[4] On this reckoning the word "dinner" would be more rapidly recognised – and cognised – than that of "break", the latter used frequently in school but only recently introduced into the child's vocabulary. It is likely that the same holds for syntactic structures and basic semantic structures, viz. that those acquired earliest, for example in stages I or II of *Fig. 11.2* would have the advantage of familiarity and imagery over those acquired in Stage V. Information on the ordering of acquisition is thus seen to be a data bank for the writing of meaningful reading materials for the beginner reader. A practical example of this would be for instance the information that the irregular form of the verb appears before the regular form; or again that the uncontractable form appears before the contractable, thus: 'They are gone,' before 'They're gone'.

To sum up the ideas I have been attempting to express in this paper:

1 The most complex and palpable skill that the young child brings to the reading task is his own language structure.
2 This skill has to be slowly grafted to other reading skills, such as isolating sounds from print, visual discrimination, blending, reading-segmentation rules.
3 Since the child is an apprentice in the reading skills but a master in language skills the latter should be allowed to play as supportive a role as possible.
4 To do this it is essential to understand where child language is "at" for the five and six-year-old child, not where we want it to go to; we must search for a match and avoid a mismatch.
5 In the search for complexity control, sentence length stands up well to scrutiny, provided we are aware of other features of the normative schedules.
6 Such normative schedules are in process of being outlined by linguists and psycholinguists.

In 1961 reading specialists, gathered at Syracuse University from all parts of the United States, decided that the area of reading instruction in greatest need of research was the first grade.[5] Considering what we have learned about child language in the ensuing sixteen years it might not be too fanciful to suggest that the area with greatest potential for first grade reading might well be that of first grade language.

References

1. Brown, R. *A first language: the early stages.* Cambridge, Mass: Harvard University Press 1973.
2. Crystal, D., Fletcher, P. and Garman, M. *The grammatical analysis of language disorders: a procedure for assessment and remediation.* London: Arnold, 1976.
3. Brown, R. and Herrnstein, R.J. *Psychology*. London, Methuen & Co. Ltd., 1975. p. 478.
4. Carroll, J.B. and White, M.N. Word frequency and age of acquisiton as determiners of picture-naming latency. *Quarterly Journal of Experimental Psychology*, 1973, 25, 85-95.
5. *Learning to Read: A Report of a Conference of Reading Experts.* Princeton, N.J. Educational Testing Service, 1962.

IV. MEASUREMENT AND READING

12. Testing Reading Tests

Fergus McBride, Moray House College of Education, Edinburgh

Some time ago a primary head teacher who had given a large group of his older pupils two different published reading tests was astonished to find that:

1. The differences in individual pupils' reading ages given by the two tests exceeded 11 months in over one-third of cases.
2. The average reading age of the pupils was 12,3 on one test and 11,7 on the other.
3. The correlation between the two sets of reading ages was 0.82 ± 2.

He had selected these tests because they appeared to meet his requirements regarding cost, administration and content, and was disillusioned by the disparity of the results. Many other less well documented reports of discrepancies in results of reading tests have been encountered.

It cannot be over-emphasised that the first consideration in selecting a reading test is the *content* of the test. The teacher must ask:

(a) Is the written material in the test typical of the sort of material I wish this pupil to be able to read?
(b) Are the tasks demanded of the pupil in doing the test typical of the tasks I wish the pupil to be able to perform?

The teacher, being a realist, will also have to consider cost, ease of administration and usefulness of the results. But the question posed by our head teacher must also be answered.

1. Are such discrepancies generally found between currently used published tests?
2. If so, to what extent are these discrepancies legitimate?
3. What effect do such discrepancies have on the uses to which the test results are put?
4. How can the discrepancies be overcome?

At the outset it must be stated that discrepancies in assessments by different tests can only be detected if the tests use the same units of measurement. Some tests use Reading Ages[1] and others provide Standarised Reading Scores.[2] Reading Ages compare the pupil's performance with the average performance of pupils of different ages, whilst S.R.S.'s compare the pupil's performance with those of the same age. It is hazardous or impossible to make comparisons between them. Both measures have advantages and disadvantages for test-user and test-conductor. Whatever the advantages appertaining to one measure used in a particular situation, obviously comparisons cannot be made with other test results unless the same units are used. But given that like can be compared with like i.e. that the units of measurement are the same, *what are the possible sources of discrepancies in the scores of the same individuals and the same groups on different reading tests?*

In the first instance lack of reliability of a test is a source. It is salutary to remember that with a reliability of 0.90 one can expect a third of the pupils' Standardised Reading Scores to be in error by 4.74 points or more and even with a reliability as high as 0.97 this figure is only reduced to 2.60. Discrepancies due to lack of reliability, therefore, are undesirable and an essential characteristic of a test is high reliability.

But although high test reliability is necessary condition for conformity of results of different tests, it is not sufficient. The electricity meter and the gas meter are each (one hopes) highly reliable but one does not expect conformity of numerical readings. One expects a low correlation between the readings. Similarly tests, even though individually reliable, will give discrepant assessments of individuals if there is a low inter-test correlation, i.e. presumably, the tests are measuring different aspects of reading ability. Unlike reliability, high inter-test correlation is not always desirable. If two tests are to be used interchangeably for 'monitoring' or 'screening' individual pupils, high I.T.C. would be essential, but if different tests (or sub-tests) are being used diagnostically i.e. to assess pupil's strengths and weaknesses in different reading abilities, then low I.T.C. would be desirable.

Finally, two tests with high reliability and high correlation between their assessments may give discrepant results because of the different standardisation samples used. Tests are necessarily 'normed' on different samples of pupils at different times and in different places. When different *mean* R.A.'s or S.R.S.'s are obtained for the same group of pupils using different Reading Tests, the reason most probably is due to this *incompatibility of norms.* However if the nature and extent of the incompatibility is known, comparisons between scores on the different tests may be made legitimately in much the same way as degrees Centigrade are converted to degrees Fahrenheit.

In summary, then, if one wishes to ascertain the discrepancies which may be expected between the assessment made by different tests one must examine:

1. The Reliabilities of the tests.
2. The Inter-Test Correlation.
3. The Compatibility of the sets of norms.

As we have seen, we often need tests with low inter-correlations e.g., sub-tests of Edinburgh Reading Tests (1). However, the norms of the various tests or sub-tests must be compatible when used conjointly for screening, monitoring or diagnostic purposes. That is, in spite of the desirably low correlation between the assessments made by the different sub-tests, the various percentile scores, for a representative group of pupils, should not differ significantly.

The effects of the degree of I.T.C. and Compatibility of Norms of different tests are illustrated in the following diagrams.

Effect of Inter-correlation of test scores and compatibility of norms on outcome of "screening" procedures using different tests.

Fig. 12.1 Illustrating perfect correlation and complete compatibility of norms.

Ten pupils given test 1 and test 2

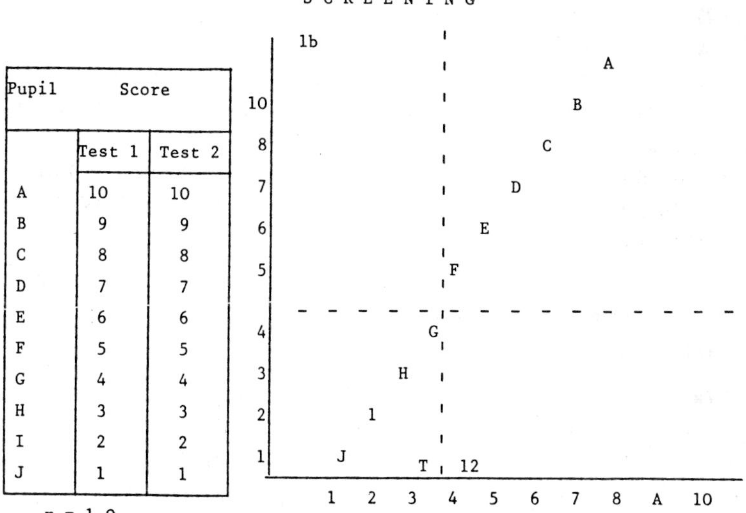

Pupil	Score	
	Test 1	Test 2
A	10	10
B	9	9
C	8	8
D	7	7
E	6	6
F	5	5
G	4	4
H	3	3
I	2	2
J	1	1

r = 1.0

Outcome: <u>The same pupils "screened" by tests 1 and 2</u>

Fig. 12.2 Illustrating perfect correlation but lack of compatibility of norms.

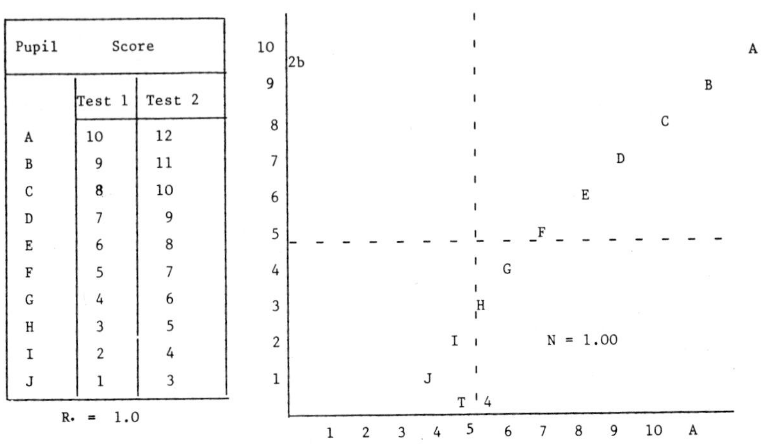

Pupil	Score	
	Test 1	Test 2
A	10	12
B	9	11
C	8	10
D	7	9
E	6	8
F	5	7
G	4	6
H	3	5
I	2	4
J	1	3

R. = 1.0

N.B. By moving y ordinate to 6½ the result is identical with Diagram 1

Fig. 12.3 Illustrating imperfect correlation but complete compatibility of norms.

The same pupils given the tests 1 and 4

Pupil	Score	
	Test 1	Test 2
A	10	9
B	9	10
C	8	8
D	7	4
E	6	2
F	5	7
G	4	6
H	3	5
I	2	1
J	1	3

RHO = 0.73

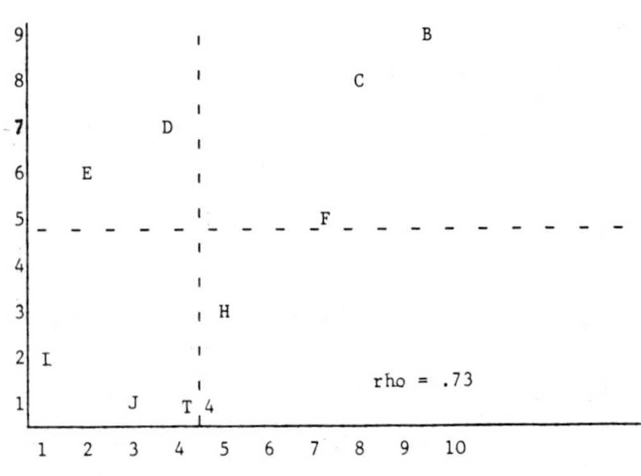

Outcome : Pupils H and G screened by Test 1 but not by Test 4.
Pupils E and D screened by Test 4 but not by Test 1.

Fig. 12.4 Illustrating imperfect correlation and lack of compatibility of norms.

The same pupils given the tests 1 and 5.

Pupil	Score	
	Test 1	Test 2
A	10	11
B	9	12
C	8	10
D	7	6
E	6	4
F	5	9
G	4	8
H	3	7
I	2	3
J	1	5

rho = 0.73

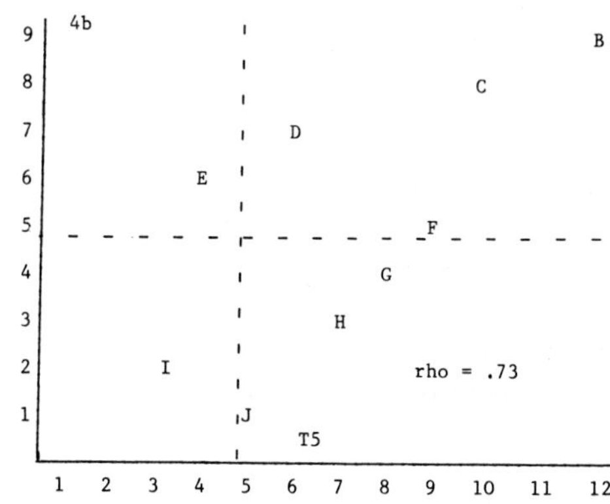

Outcome : Pupil E screened by Test 5 but not by Test 1.
Pupils G, H and J screened by Test 1 but not by Test 5.

N.B. By moving the Y ordinate to 6½ the result is identical with Diagram 3.

A Survey

During 1977 the author made two separate field studies in Scotland of these three features of several currently published tests with 750 pupils aged 10,0 to 12,6 in normal classes and 260 pupils aged 12,0 to 13,6 in "Remedial" classes in Secondary Schools. The samples of pupils were made as representative as possible of pupils in Scotland in general and the sequencing and timing of the administration of the tests was arranged in such a way as to offset practice and fatigue effects.

The tests studied were:

With 10,0 to 12,6 group

Edinburgh Reading Test, Stage 3. (E.R.T.3)	(1973)
National Foundation, Test DE. (N.F.D.E.)	(1974)
Schonell Silent Reading Test, R4 (S.R.4)	(1955)
Richmond Test of Reading Comprehensive Levels 3 and 4 (R.L.3, R.L. 4)	(1975)

With the 12,0 to 13,6 group

Schonell Silent Reading Test, R.4. (S.R.4)	(1955)
Richmond Test of Reading Comprehension Level 1. (R.L.1)	(1975)
Gap Reading Comprehension Test Form R (Red) and Form N (Blue). (G.R. G.B.)	(1970)
Daniels and Diack Reading Test 12. (D.D.2)	(1958)

The Consistency (or Reliability) of the Tests

The reliabilities of the tests with each group were calculated using the Kuder-Richardson Formula 20.

From the reliability co-efficient it is possible to calculate the extent of error to be expected in an individual score using the formula S.E. = $\sigma\sqrt{1 - r}$ where σ is the standard deviation of the test scores and r is the reliability coefficient of the test. When S.E. has been calculated we can predict that 32 per cent of scores will be in error by more than 1 S.E.

The KR.20 Reliabilities were found to be:

With the 10,0 to 12,6 group:

	KR.20	S.E.
Edinburgh Reading Test, 3.	0.97	2.55
National Foundation Test, D.E.	0.93	3.97
Schonell Silent Reading Test, R.4	0.92	* –
Richmond Test, Level 3.	0.91	4.50
Richmond Test, Level 4.	0.91	4.50

With the 12,0 to 13,6 group:

	KR.20	S.E.
Schonell Test, R.4	0.87	*–
Richmond Test, Level 1	0.92	3.57
Gap (Red) Test	0.84	*–
Gap (Blue) Test	0.83	*–
Daniels & Diack, Test 12	0.98	*–

*These tests provide assessments in terms of reading ages so standard errors are not given.

In fact the units of measurement used by each test are:

	Reading Ages	*S.R.S.*
ERT, 3	X	X
NF, DE.		X
Schonell R4	X	
Richmond Tests		X
Gap Tests	X	
Daniels & Diack	X	

Comment on Reliabilities of Tests

The S.E.'s show the extent of the error to be expected in an individual score and from the above table it is clear that for monitoring and screening satisfactorily, reliabilities of 0.95 and over are highly desirable. From the item analyses carried out on these tests in these trials it is clear that reliability could be increased by the replacement of items which do not measure up to accepted standards in respect of facility and discrimination values.

For example: With the 10,0 to 12,6 age group, the Schonell, R.4 Test, 10 of the 42 items in the test had facility values of 85 per cent or over and the average f.v. for all items was 78.40.

For the 12,0 to 13,6 group (Remedial), only the Richmond Test, L1 had a satisfactory reliability (0.92), but norms are not available for this age group for this Test.

Fig. 12.5 Reading ages (in months) of 130 secondary school pupils aged 12,0 to 13,6 in remedial classes as given by Schonell, R.4 silent reading test and the Gap. (Blue) test (intercorrelation 0.612).

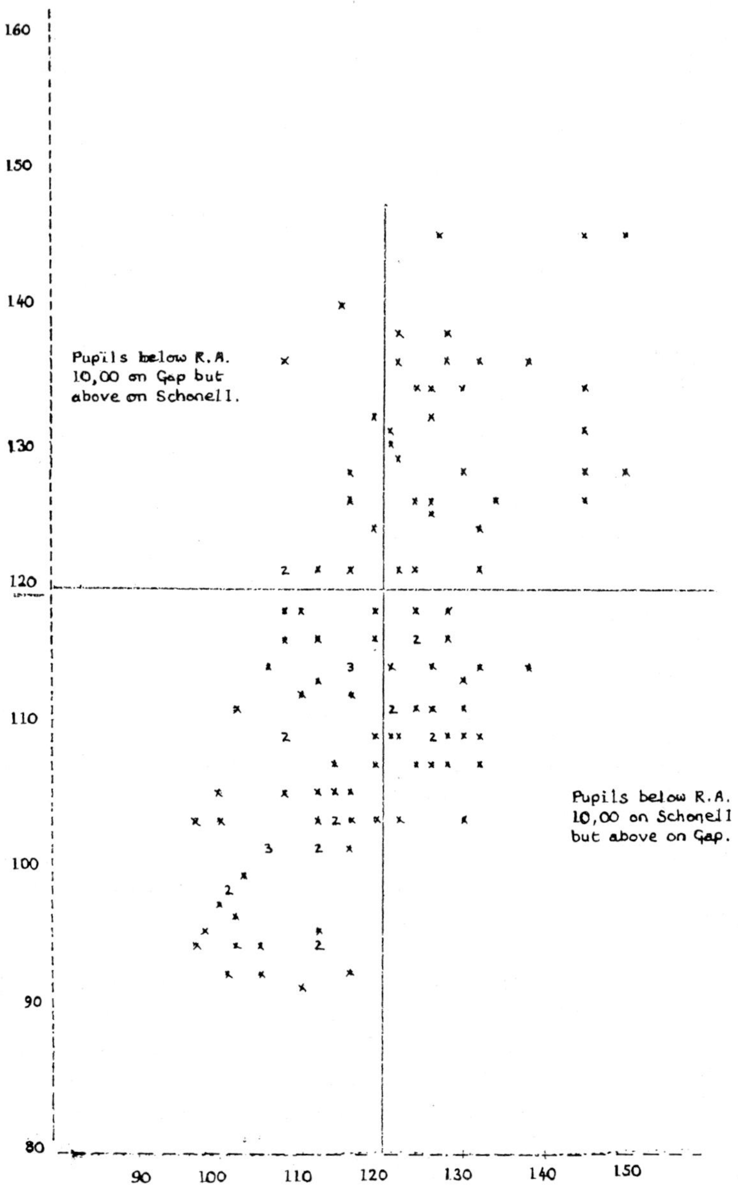

Inter-Test Correlation (I.T.C.)

The following I.T.C.'s were found in the two groups of pupils:

With the 10,0 to 12,6 age group:

	R.L.3	R.L.4	S.R.4	N.F.D.E.
E.R.T. 3	0.86	0.85	0.82	0.90
S.R. 4	0.79	0.64		

With the 12,0 to 13,6 age group: (Remedial)

	R.L.1	S.R.4	Gap(R)	Gap(B)	D & D
R.L.1	–	0.63	0.51	0.63	0.57
S.R.4	0.63	–	0.69	0.63	0.65
Gap(R)	0.51	0.69	–	–	0.70
Gap(B)	0.63	0.63	–	–	0.60
D & D	0.57	0.65	0.70	0.60	–
Mean	0.58	0.65	0.63	0.62	0.63

Comment on I.T.C.'s

Low I.T.C. between two tests means little correspondence between a pupil's scores on the two separate tests even when administered with the utmost care. Therefore, to use two different tests with low I.T.C. (say 0.60 to 0.70) interchangeably for monitoring or screening pupils is only about 25 per cent better than picking scores out of a hat. Yet for the older (Remedial) group the I.T.C.'s are between 0.51 and 0.70. The discrepancies in the results from two different tests are clearly shown in the scatter diagram below.

From these diagrams the reader can work out for himself the discrepancies in an individual's scores or in pupils screened, which occur from using any pair of the tests named on the scatter diagrams.

It is certain that these low I.T.C.'s are largely accounted for by the low reliabilities of the tests, especially with the 12,0 to 13,6 (Remedial) group. These considerations would point to the conclusion that unless there is high I.T.C. between the Tests used, monitoring and screening should be carried out with the test only.

Compatibility of Norms

Tables 12.1, 12.2 and 12.3 below show the standarised reading scores given by the different tests for the same representative groups of pupils ages between 10,0 and 12,6 at different percentile points.

Table 12.4 below shows the reading ages given by the different tests for the group of 12,0 to 13,6 pupils (Remedial) at different percentile points. The reader will be able to work out from these Diagrams and Tables the extent of the discrepancies in assessments of pupils at different levels of performance. Most of the differences are statistically significant.

Table 12.1 Sample: 232 pupils aged 10,0 to 12,6

	Percentiles								
Test	10th	20th	30th	40th	50th	60th	70th	80th	90th
E.R.T. 3	77	84	88	92	94	100	105	109	117
N.F.E.R. D.E.	84	89	93	97	99	102	106	112	119

$r = 0.86 \pm 0.017$

Table 12.2 Sample: 223 pupils aged 11,5 to 12,6

	Percentiles								
Test	10th	20th	30th	40th	50th	60th	70th	80th	90th
E.S.T. 3	80	89	93	96	99	101	105	110	116
Richmond L.4.	82	90	94	100	104	104	108	114	121

$r = 0.85 \pm 0.018$

Table 12.3 Sample: 216 pupils aged 10,0 to 11,4

	Percentiles								
Test	10th	20th	30th	40th	50th	60th	70th	80th	90th
E.R.T.3	80	85	90	93	98	103	106	110	119
Richmond L.4	83	89	95	98	101	106	110	114	122

$r = 0.86 \pm 0.020$

Table 12.4 *Reading age equivalents for the four tests, at different percentiles. Sample: 260 pupils aged 12,0 to 13,6 (Remedial)*

	No.	Mean		S.D.		Percentiles																	
						10th		20th		30th		40th		50th		60th		70th		80th		90th	
		Yr	Mt	Yr	Mt	Yr	Mt	Yr	Mt	Yr	Mt	Yr	Mt	Yr	Mt	Yr	Mt	Yr	Mt	Yr	Mt	Yr	Mt
Schonell	285	9	4	1	2	7	11	8	5	8	7	9	1	9	3	9	6	10	0	10	6	11	2
Gap Red	132	9	6	1	0	8	5	8	7	8	11	9	1	9	4	9	10	10	3	10	5	10	11
Gap Blue	130	9	11	0	11	8	6	9	0	9	4	9	8	9	11	10	2	10	6	10	8	11	0
D and D	258	9	3	1	5	7	6	7	11	8	5	8	10	9	1	9	5	10	0	10	0	11	2
Richmond	267	9	4	1	10	7	3	7	6	8	0	8	7	9	6	—	—	—	—	—	—	—	—

Comments on Compatibility of Norms

Clearly, in the case of both groups the norms of the tests studied are incompatible and to an increased degree, for pupils of average and below average performance.

Therefore, to use different tests interchangeably for screening or monitoring procedures without evidence of the compatibility of norms is a hazardous exercise. However, other considerations being satisfactory, provided that the extent of the discrepancies in norms are known, procedures for "equating" norms can be applied to tests when used interchangeably for screening and monitoring operations.

The Diagnostic or Analytic use of Tests

In a general sense, tests are used diagnostically when they provide information on the extent and nature of pupils' abilities in reading and, therefore, useful in planning teaching procedures.

Tests used for "screening" provide information which is useful for organising teaching and tests used for "monitoring" throw light upon the effectiveness of the teaching provided.

But the teacher is demanding more than these procedures provide. He asks "What skills and competencies do I need to help this pupil to acquire in order that he will become a better reader?" – which raises the vital questions, "What are the Components of Reading Ability?" and "Which of these does this particular pupil need to be taught?" Clearly the answer to the former is that the skills required are different at different stages and there are still wide differences of opinion as to what these are. The second question cannot be answered without answering the first.

Nevertheless, every Reading Test is based upon some answer to the key question above as to what constitutes reading ability and a pupil's score on a particular test (within the limitation already discussed) provides a measure of his competence in the processes which the test maker has deemed to constitute at least some part or indication of Reading Ability, e.g., recognition of words, completion of sentences, answering questions and so on. In this respect the tests are 'diagnostic'.

The only test studied which was originally intended to be 'diagnostic', in the sense that it was designed to measure pupils' strengths and weaknesses in different types of reading undertaken normally by pupils 10,0 to 12,6, was the Edinburgh Reading Test, Stage 3. This consisted of 5 sub-tests and provided a profile of performance as well as an overall Reading Quotient (or Standardised Reading Score) and a Reading Age within the 10,0 to 12,6 range.

In this experiment the Reliabilities of the sub-tests of the E.R.T. 3 range from 0.85 to 0.94 (overall 0.97) which makes each sub-test comparable to a reading test in its own right.

The I.T.C.'s of the E.R.T. sub-tests varied from 0.70 to 0.82. For diagnostic purposes these should be as low as possible and these I.T.C.'s are as low as has been achieved by other tests of the same nature.

Some authorities believe that the higher the correlation between the sub-test scores the less sensitive the sub-test scores to differences between them[3,4] but the conclusion that because of inter-correlations of the order of 0.70 to 0.80 the sub-tests are 'measuring the same skill' is unjustified. Measurements of the height and weight of persons are highly correlated but one does not conclude that the measurements are of the same quality. The measurements are rather of *different* qualities which are related.

The findings in this study justify the procedures outlined in the Manual[5] for screening pupils with usually high or low sub-test procedures, and also for using the tests for determining the strengths and weaknesses of a class as a whole.

In conclusion, we can sum up by answering the Headmaster's original four questions:

Answer 1: Discrepancies are found between assessments by different Reading Tests.

Answer 2: Undesirable discrepancies occur as the result of imperfect reliability and imcompatibility of test norms.

Discrepancies due to low inter-test correlation may be welcome for diagnostic purposes.

Answer 3: (a) Unreliability is undesirable for all testing purposes.

(b) High inter-test correlation is desirable when

tests are used interchangeably for monitoring and screening purposes. Low inter-test correlation is desirable when tests are used interchangeably for monitoring screening or diagnostic purposes.

Answer 4: (a) Unreliability is determined in the course of construction of the test.

(b) Inter-test correlation is not always desirable.

(c) Norms for different tests may be equated statistically.

References and Bibliography

1. Bookbinder, G.E. Reading Ages and Standardised Scores. *Reading*, 1976, 10-3, 20.24.
2. Pilliner, A.E.G. and Reid, J.F. – in Reid, J.F., (Ed.) *Reading: Problems and Practices.* London: Ward Lock Educational, 1972.
3. Daniels, J.C. and Diack, H. *The Standard Reading Tests.* London: Chatto and Windus, 1958.
4. *Edinburgh Reading Tests.* London: Hodder and Stoughton, 1972.
5. McBride, J.F. and McNaught, P.C. *Manual of Instructions, Edinburgh Reading Tests, Stage 3.* London: Hodder and Stoughton, 1972.
6. *Reading Comprehension Test, D.E.*, London: National Foundation for Education Research, 1974.
7. *Richmond Tests of Basic Skills.* London: Thomas Nelson and Sons Ltd., 1975.
8. Schonell, F.J., *Silent Reading Test, B.* (Test R4) Edinburgh: Oliver & Boyd, 1955.

13. Research on the Assessment of Pre-reading Skills – an American Perspective

Joanne R. Nurss, Georgia State University, Atlanta, Georgia

This paper traces the history of readiness testing in America showing its close relationship to intelligence testing. It describes current readiness tests, the areas covered (visual and auditory skills, comprehension of oral language, and observational data on language skills and reading interest), and score information provided. It also discusses future trends from research such as the closer link of instruction and assessment and the assessment of a child's concepts of language. Finally, implications for classroom teachers are given. Central to the paper is the idea of using prereading skills assessment data to answer the questions: readiness for what? taught how? with which materials? by whom?

Historical Perspective

The assessment of prereading skills or reading readiness in America began in the late 1920s as an out-growth of the measurement movement. In the early 1930s Gertrude Hildreth published the first edition of the *Metropolitan Readiness Tests.* Other early readiness tests included the *Lee-Clark Reading Readiness Test* and the *Gates Reading Readiness Test.* These tests were primarily an assessment of the child's visual and oral vocabulary skills. They were group-administered, paper-and-pencil tests and followed the best measurement principles developed at that time. They were seen as measures of cognitive functioning or mental abilities whose purpose was to predict school readiness. In her book, *Readiness for School Beginner,*[1] Hildreth gives the purpose of such measures by saying: "Readiness tests are useful to teachers in helping to describe and compare the traits of individual pupils, and to school administrators in indicating the range of ability and knowledge among all the school entrants in a school or within the school system" (p.64). Readiness tests were to "discriminate among the ready and less ready and to screen out those most certain to fail" (p. 64). This screening out or prediction of failure was one of the major functions of readiness tests. Because intelligence tests also showed the child's potential for school learning (that is, predicted success or failure), they were classified as readiness measures.[1] This linking of readiness and intelligence was strengthened by the research of Morphett and Washburne who found that a mental age of 6.5 years was necessary for learning to read.[2] Their concept of readiness and readiness assessment was prevalent for several decades among American educators in spite of a group of research studies completed by Gates (1936-7) which led him to suggest that there might not be a necessary mental age for learning to read. In fact, Gates suggested that readiness must be assessed in relation to the methods and materials that will be used for instruction. This idea was largely ignored for the next 30-35 years.

In the period of the 1940s through the 1960s the major purpose of readiness tests was to use the total score for prediction of success or failure and to place the children into groups for readiness instruction. Typically, 6 to 8 weeks of readiness instruction was provided in which the children often completed one or more readiness workbooks. The purpose of this readiness period was social and physical adjustment to school; visual and auditory discrimination training; development of language facility and background experiences; learning to recognise colours, read pictures, and demonstrate left-to-right orientation; and gaining motivation to learn to read.[3] Readiness instruction was seen as involving a number of factors, but was not directly related to the specific instructional method that would be used to teach reading, nor was it directly related to the readiness test results.

In the early 1960s Durkin completed two research studies

which indicated that some children were entering first grade already reading,[4] a fact not identified by the readiness tests. As a result of this research, she called for a rethinking of the concept of readiness away from that of a product resulting from maturation toward that of a process evolving as children interact with their environment. Readiness as related to the instructional materials to be used in beginning reading is becoming a more common theme in the research of the 1970s. MacGinitie takes us back to Gates' earlier notions (1936-7) saying that the relevant question is not "Is the child ready to read?", but rather "readiness for what? how?"[5] Ausubel[6] had earlier defined readiness in this same vein stating that readiness is "the adequacy of existing capacity in relation to the demands of a given learning task" (p. 247). Wanat suggests that readiness tests ought to be concerned with modifying the learning environment, not just the learning.[7] The concept of readiness or prereading skills assessment has changed from assessment of the child's developmental probability of success or failure in reading, to an assessment of the child's skill development in relation to the reading instructional environment.

Current Status

Most current readiness tests reflect these newer concepts at least to some degree. The emphasis is on skills related to beginning reading, usually in the areas of decoding and comprehension. The decoding skills measured fall into two groups – visual and auditory skills. Research by Barrett indicates that visual discrimination of letters and words, visual memory, and letter recognition are all related to success in beginning reading.[8] Goins adds figure-ground perception and visual closure to that list.[9] Hall[10] notes that early writing activities (usually assessed in a prereading skills test by a measure of visual-motor coordination) are related to beginning reading success also.[10] The current prereading skills measures all include subtests in at least some of these areas. McNinch and Richmond found that auditory discrimination of sounds, auditory memory, auditory blending, and auditory-visual integration all were significant factors in accounting for end-of-first grade reading achievement.[11] Current tests usually include some auditory subtests, with auditory-visual integration being measured by a test of sound-letter correspondence. Comprehension skills include measures of oral language (vocabulary, and concepts), listening and reasoning, and language structure. Smith[12] and Gibson and Levin[13] emphasise that the successful reader must predict or extract meaning from the printed page. Oral language, based directly upon the child's experiences is the best indicator of the child's success in so doing. Because oral vocabulary is so culturally linked, several current tests are omitting this measure from the prereading skills battery.

Skills thought to be important to beginning reading success, but not easily measured in a group, paper-and-pencil test, are usually included in some kind of observation checklist. Clymer and Barrett include oral language, social skills, emotional development, attitude toward and interest in learning to read, and work habits in their rating scale.[14]

Recently, a number of criterion-referenced tests have been published. These relate to a group of other children (norm group). These measures have the advantage of being able to be directly linked to a specific curriculum of a school system or state or to specific materials available from a particular publisher. They seem to be a logical choice for a prereading skills test based on the current idea of relating assessment to instruction. Unfortunately, however, very little attention has been given to the reliability or validity of such measures, especially those designed to accompany a series of basal readers. If a test is not reliable, the score is, of course, meaningless. The publishers of such tests need to establish the reliabilities of their tests, include them in the manuals, and work to improve them if they are low.

Recent Findings

Some recent research findings are providing new ideas for inclusion in current and future readiness tests. Until recently, almost every study completed indicated that the single best predictor of end-of-first-grade reading achievement was knowledge of letter names.[15] A recent study by Mitchell completed in connection with the revision of the *Metropolitan Readiness Tests*, shows that pupils entering first grade have already mastered the names of the letters of the alphabet.[16] If a letter recognition test is too easy for entering first graders, it will no longer predict end-of-first-grade reading achievement. Readiness tests designed to be given at the end of kindergarten or the beginning of first grade will no longer include a letter recognition test. This does not mean that all children beginning first grade will know all the letters of the alphabet. The teacher will want to do a screening of letter knowledge with each child in the class.

Earlier versions of readiness tests used non-language symbols to assess auditory and visual discrimination. Sounds from the environment, pictures, geometric symbols, shapes, and designs, all were used. Recent research indicates that assessment of skills related to reading is accomplished by the use of actual symbols; that is, letter sounds (phonemes), letters (graphemes), and letter-like artificial symbols.[8] If one were interested in assessing the children's visual discrimination skills with no possibility of learning from the environment interfering, it would be best to use artificial letter symbols; otherwise a prereading test of visual discrimination should use letters and numerals.

The trend toward making prereading skills tests more related to instruction has led to a de-emphasis on the total score (except for certain research purposes) and the inclusion of part scores in most prereading tests. In order for the part or subtest scores to be used, two criteria must be met. First, the parts or subtests, whichever are to be used, must be reliable enough to be used alone. Frequently, these are short tests and, therefore, may not have high reliability. Secondly, the intercorrelations between the subtests or areas must be low enough to indicate that they are measuring different skills, at least in part. Scheuneman did a factor analysis of the *Metropolitan Readiness Tests* and concluded that the data supported providing area scores on those tests.[17]

Research in the 1960s made test authors aware of the effect of cultural and environmental differences on the child's test performance. Current tests are taking steps to reduce test bias against children from any particular socio-economic level, cultural or ethnic group, sex, geographical region, or language background.[18] In addition to modifying the tests themselves, 'many prereading skills' measures now include a test-taking skill or practice exercise. The children are given instructions in the vocabulary necessary to succeed in the test; for example, "row", "column", "same", "different", and so on. They are also introduced to the item formats used in the text, given practice in the marking system, and allowed to work in small groups under test-like conditions. Obviously, this type of instruction and practice means that children who have never been to school before and who have had little exposure to pencils and books are given a fairer chance to succeed on the test than if they had been tested "cold."

Another trend is toward the reduction of the verbal memory load in readiness tests. Jones found the memory load on tests of listening comprehension and following oral directions to be particularly high.[19] Recent tests have minimised this problem by having oral directions or long comprehension items repeated by the examiner.

Future Directions for Prereading Measures

The past few years have seen a growing body of research on the child's understanding of language concepts and of the reading process itself. Similar studies have been completed in the United States, Canada, and England. In one study children were asked to segment oral and written contexts into words. Kindergarteners were unable to do so by conventional word boundaries.[20] Other research indicates that preschool children do not understand the meaning of the concepts "reading", "word", or "letter."[21, 22] Further research is needed to understand the relationship of these concepts to learning to read. It is likely that a test of language concepts might contribute to a test of pre-reading skills.

Future pre-reading skills measures are likely also to include an assessment of the child's skills in word recognition or actual reading. This could be accomplished either by a traditional subtest of these skills or by an instructional/testing task in which the children are taught a few words and a short time later tested on their recognition and understanding of the words in context. This kind of subtest would help identify children who may already know how to read and would give the teacher valuable information about the child's learning patterns and styles.

Implications for Classroom Teachers

The implications of the prereading assessment research discussed in this paper extend quite broadly to classroom teachers. One of the major concerns of teachers needs to be in the selection of a pre-reading test to use in their classrooms. If the school system selection team does not include teachers, a valuable source of input is lost and the danger of misinterpretation and inefficient use of the test results is increased. Teachers selecting the readiness test must look for the test's reliability and validity. They must decide if they are seeking a norm-referenced or a criterion-referenced measure. They must determine if a practice test is included and if the scores are relatively free from bias. Finally they must assess the possible relationship of the instrument to their reading/language arts curriculum. For example, do the skill scores provide information with which the teacher can modify a given child's beginning reading curriculum?

Another implication for the oral classroom teacher is in planning instructionally-related assessment tasks to follow up the information gained from the prereading skills test. For example, if a child scored low on a test of sound-letter correspondences, the teacher might try one or two games (with the child) which afford an opportunity to observe whether the child can discriminate between sounds and can recognise the name letters (both prerequisite skills to learning sound-letter correspondence). If not, the child's instruction would begin in these areas. If the child had no difficulty with these tasks, instruction in sound-letter correspondences would begin.

To assist the classroom teacher as much as possible, future readiness tests must bring about a closer relationship between assessment and instruction. As Durkin[4] has pointed out, readiness is a process that develops within the child's environment. The purpose of readiness assessment is not to obtain a score with which the child can be labelled and with which the child's first grade achievement can be perfectly predicted. Rather the purpose of readiness assessment is to provide the teacher with specific instructional data about each child's skill level so that the prediction of the test may be ruined! The questions the teacher should be asking are readiness for what? taught how? with which materials? by whom?

References and Bibliography

1. Hildreth, G.H. *Readiness for School Beginners.* New York: World Book Co., 1950.
2. Morphett, M and Washburne, C. When should children begin to read? *Elementary School Journal,* 1931, 31, 496-503.
3. Tinker, M. and McCullough, C. *Teaching Elementary Reading.* (2nd Ed.) New York: Appleton-Century-Crofts, Inc., 1962.
4. Durkin, D. When should children begin to read? In H.M. Robinson (Ed.), Innovation and change in reading instruction. *Yearbook for the National Society for the Study of Education,* 1967, 67, Part II, 30-71.
5. MacGinitie, W.H., Evaluating readiness for learning to read: a critical review of evaluation and research. *Reading Research Quarterly,* 1969, 4, 396-410.
6. Ausubel, D.P. Viewpoint from related disciplines: human growth and development. *Teachers College Record,* 1959, 60, 245-54.
7. Wanat, S.F. Reading Readiness. *Visible Language,* 1976, 10, 101-27.
8. Barrett, T.C. The relationship between measures of prereading visual discrimination and first grade reading achievement: a review of the literature. *Reading Research Quarterly,* 1965, I, 51-76.
9. Goins, J.T. Visual perceptual abilities and early reading progress. *University of Chicago Supplemental Educational Monographs,* 1958, No. 87.
10. Hall, M.A. Prereading instruction: teach for the task. *Reading Teacher,* 1976, 30, 7-9.
11. McNinch, G. and Richmond, M. Auditory perceptual tasks as predictors of first grade reading success. *Perceptual and Motor Skills,* 1972, 35, 7-13.
12. Smith, F. *Comprehension and Learning: A Conceptual Framework for Teachers.* New York: Holt, Rinehart, Winston, 1975.
13. Gibson, E.J. and Levin, H. *The Psychology of Reading.* Cambridge, Mass.: Massachusetts Institute of Technology Press, 1975.
14. Clymer, T. & Barrett, T.C. *Clymer-Barrett Prereading Battery.* Lexington, Mass.: Personnel Press, 1968.
15. Muehl, S. and Nello, M.C. Early first-grade skills related to subsequent reading performances: a seven-year follow-up. *Journal of Reading Behavior,* 1976, 8, 67-81.
16. Mitchell, B.C. *Changes over an eight- and nine-year period in the*

readiness level of entering first-grade pupils. Paper presented at the meeting of the National Council on Measurement in Education, Chicago, April, 1974.

17. Sheuneman, J. *Maximum Likelihood Factor Analysis.* Unpublished report, Harcourt, Brace, Jovanovich, Inc., 1975.
18. Nurss, J.R. An attempt to reduce test bias in readiness tests. In R.C. Granger & J.C. Young (Eds.), *Demythologising the Inner-City Child.* Washington, D.C.: National Association for the Education of Young Children, 1976, pp. 33-6.
19. Jones, M.H. *The Unintentional Memory Load in Tests for Young Children.* (Center for the Study of Evaluation, Report No. 57.) Los Angeles: University of California at Los Angeles, 1970.
20. Holden, M.H. and MacGinitie, W.H. Children's conceptions of word boundaries in speech and print. *Journal of Educational Psychology*, 1972, 63, 551-7.
21. Oliver, M.E. The development of language concepts of pre-primary Indian children. *Language Arts*, 1975, 52, 865-9.
22. Downing, J., Ollila, L., & Oliver, P. Cultural differences in children's concepts of reading and writing. *British Journal of Educational Psychology*, 1975, 45, 312-6.
23. Gates, A.I. *Gates Reading Readiness Test.* New York: Bureau of Publications, Teachers' College, Columbia University.
24. Lee, J.M. & Clark, W.W. *Lee-Clark Reading Readiness Test.* Los Angeles: California Test Bureau.

V. ADULT LITERACY

14. *Aspects of Adult Literacy Teaching in Ireland*

Rev. Liam Carey, Adult and Community Education Department, St. Patrick's College, Maynooth

Illiteracy is a fact in Ireland today. There are adults between the ages of 16 and 80 years of age, men and women, who can neither read nor write nor use basic numeracy skills. A cursory investigation of the many literacy programmes now in progress and an analysis of the numbers of letters received as a result of the recent Radio Telefis Eireann radio programme entitled "Helping Adults to Read", revealed that there are about 3,500 adults, who have literacy problems. But I believe this is the tip of the illiteracy iceberg. The full extent and nature of this problem has not yet been clearly identified. This would seem to me to be a basic requirement and the priority for the development of a national literacy campaign.

The problem of adult illiteracy was first mentioned in the *Interim Report on Adult Education in Ireland*, published in 1969.[1] This Interim Report, which was meant to stimulate community and institutional reactions regarding the nature of future structures of the adult education provision in Ireland, stressed that adult illiteracy existed here and should be given priority in any relevant and meaningful adult education provision in this country. There were reactions to this statement. The institutional reaction, in many cases, was to deny that the problem existed. The Economic and Social Research Institute however, supported the assertion that adult illiteracy existed in this country. Some of the research, undertaken by this Institute in the area of vocational development, and attitudes to education, indicated that many adults lacked these basic literacy competencies and thus were, or at least felt that they were inadequate, and unable to cope with their vocational demands.

The National Adult Education Committee subsequently sought to clarify its earlier statement in the Interim Report. It planned to undertake, in co-operation with the Economic and Social Research Institute, a small research project to identify the extent of adult illiteracy in Ireland. This research project, however, was not launched due to the lack of financial support. And so, the Final Report of the Committee[2] stressed again the existence of an adult illiteracy problem and urged again that it be given priority in the development of adult and community education in Ireland.

Meanwhile, the Dublin Institute of Adult Education has established a class in Basic English for Adults. The Institute, with financial support from the Dublin Vocational Education Committee (the local educational authority) commenced a literacy project. Employing a full-time director who had been involved in literacy work in London, the Institute went on to recruit voluntary tutors. These tutors received some training in how to teach reading and writing and were then matched with the illiterate adults. This agency also stimulated other agencies – statutory bodies, community groups, voluntary organisations, and individuals, to initiate literacy schemes for adults in various parts of the country. From my own research (unpublished), it would seen that about 39 different adult literacy schemes, catering for between 8 and 20 students each are now in operation. Some are staffed by a part-time organiser and small number of voluntary tutors. About six agencies employ one or more full-time organiser/trainers to administer their literacy schemes; these are the Dublin Institute of Adult Education, the Altrusa Club, Cork, the Co. Waterford V.E.C., Waterford City V.E.C., and Co. Meath V.E.C. Other Vocational Education Committees have included the task of developing a local literacy scheme in the job description of their part-time adult education officer, who, it is expected, will be the holder of a post of responsibility in the larger vocational schemes in several parts of the country.

There is no national co-ordination of adult literacy work in Ireland, nor have criteria been established whereby the work of existing literacy agencies may be assessed.[1] Yet such an assessment would be invaluable in planning a comprehensive national campaign. This assessment would attempt to evaluate the literacy activities of each agency and the planned and unplanned outcomes of literacy activities. It could monitor the recruitment, training and deployment of literacy tutors; the effectiveness of the work of the organisers and of the deployment of all resources; the relationship between voluntarism, professionalism and the achievement of literacy objectives. Above all it should identify the major problems experienced by illiterate students and the tutors and organisers especially in relation to resources and community attitudes.

Since this paper was presented, the National Adult Literacy Agency was established in 1980. The aim of this agency is to advance adult literacy in Ireland. The many objectives of N.A.L.A. include the promotion of co-operation among all those engaged in adult literacy work in Ireland, viz. the agency, the organiser, the tutor and the adult learner. N.A.L.A. publishes a regular newsletter and sponsors national conferences etc. on adult literacy problems.

Literacy work in Ireland today is almost entirely voluntary. The voluntary tutor gives his/her time, service, skill, resources and sometimes home, in order to establish a learning dialogue of hope, trust, confidence, support and love with the adult illiterate.

Who are the students?

The majority, (71 per cent) of students are males; about 50 per cent of these are married. The majority of women participants are housewives. Nearly 85 per cent of the male and female participants have either left school or dropped out prematurely at the primary school level. Whilst the male participants come from the unskilled and semi-skilled worker groups, some are also unemployed or self-employed, and even a few professional workers are included. Again, the majority of those known are found in the 20 to 38 years age group.

They tend to attribute their literacy problems to overcrowded classes in their school days; poor teaching experienced at school; lack of educational stimulation in the home; lack of special techniques of teaching for slow learners; poor school attendance and personal social problems (broken homes etc.).

Reasons for participation in literacy classes

The students claim that they attend literacy classes because they want more effectively to:

(i) communicate with their children and understand what their children are studying at school,
(ii) cope with life,
(iii) relate to married partner,
(iv) obtain promotion at work.

These assertions seem to be in harmony with the assertion of Sohan Singh:

> . . . . . .experience has shown that, the more functionally unified the diverse elements in a literacy course are, the greater is the instructional potential of the course. And the potential is heightened if the course probes an area of immediate concern to the learner.[3]

But such findings also indicate the different levels of expectation which participants have when they take part in literacy programmes. The above statement reflects the participants' concern for their own development as adults, workers, and members of families. They seem to indicate a desire and hope to become involved in the affairs of life, to change as it affects their lives. They are seeking self-fulfilment as indviduals and as members of society.

But they are shy, embarrassed, and have been unsuccessful, or at least labelled as such by society. Thus there is a high drop-out rate among these students. Nobody has investigated this problem. Is it due to their own lack of motivation, bad teaching methods, lack of feedback and positive reinforcement of their success in learning? Perhaps the learning situation is not 'psychologically safe' for the adult illiterate learners. Is he/she afraid to make mistakes? Or is the pace set by tutors too fast for the learner? Are inadequate or irrelevant teaching materials or resources used? Some students, after achieving success in the one-to-one situation move on into a class or group to study Basic English.

The Tutors

The majority (96 per cent) of the tutors are volunteers. Most are married (80 per cent) and are housewives (75 per cent). Each tutor works at least 2 hours a week alone with the student. In addition, the tutor spends some time preparing for this learning encounter. Many of the tutors will have received some basic training, perhaps 4 to 6 sessions. The basic training is usually concerned with identifying both the need and resources, and with methods of teaching reading and writing. There is little in-service training of the voluntary tutors but where it exists, in-service training may take the form of meetings, conferences etc. or the use of books, journals or television as resources for the tutor.

St. Patrick's College, Maynooth, a constituent college of the National University of Ireland, held two National Workshops on Literacy in 1977. Ninety literacy workers (organisers and tutors) attended these workshops. Subsequently, they requested the Adult and Community Education Department in the College to organise a special training course for trainers, who in turn would train the voluntary tutors in local schemes. Twenty-five literacy workers participated in this training course which continued for three residential week-ends. This programme has now been completed. As a result, nineteen new adult literacy schemes are being organised in different parts of the country. The trainers have also come together to assess available resources and to make their own materials.

Numeracy

It is significant that most of the literacy schemes for adults in Ireland do not concern themselves with developing numeracy skills in people who need them, although numeracy is generically a literacy skill.

"Numbers are indeed a language system. Arithmetic, as an expression of this language, has its own words and sentences." In 1977 Shirley Williams, Secretary of State for Education, England, urged those engaged in Adult Literacy Work to undertake projects in the field of numeracy.

Again the Department of Adult and Community Education at St. Patrick's College, recently organised a special workshop on the theme 'Numeracy in Ireland' with Dr. Versluys as consultant. One of the facts which emerged from this workshop was that there is little or no evidence of the nature or extent of the adult numeracy problem in Ireland. A few case studies based on real evidence were presented but these were insufficient evidence. It was agreed that a first priority in numeracy work in Ireland is to identify and clarify the numeracy needs of the adult students. This is now being done by using an adaptable questionnaire and case study methodology.

Special Concern Groups of Students

There are some special groups of adults, who must be the concern of those who are involved in adult literacy in Ireland today. I refer to:

(a) Adults who are seeking industrial training or retraining,
(b) Itinerants or the Travelling People,
(c) Prisoners,
(d) Unemployed and disadvantaged young adults between ages 18 and 25 years.

Adults who are seeking industrial training or retraining

During the last two years there have been two research projects, directly concerned with the literacy problem among adults who are seeking and presenting themselves for training and/or retraining. The National Industrial Training Authority (An Chomhairle Oiliuna or AnCO) is the principal semi-state agency, charged with responsibility for providing training and retraining for such groups of adults. As this agency has been continually expanding training for work schemes, it was obliged to identify the reading, writing and numeracy levels (and items) associated with the skills and jobs for which adults were being trained. Once again the functionality of literacy is stressed in this positive approach by the Authority. This agency is also anxious to discover the literacy skills (defined comprehensively) of those who do come forward for training and retraining. Indeed the agency wishes to include in this target group all disadvantaged workers, not only those who have literacy problems but those with other physical, emotional and psychological disadvantages. AnCO aims to provide an appropriate and comprehensive technical training for all groups of workers.

AnCO also appointed a research fellow to estimate, in precise terms, the literacy demands of industrial jobs at semi-skilled, skilled and first-line supervision levels, and to consider and advise on training implications. This research project has been completed but has not yet been published. Early results bear out the work of Sohan Singh in his listing of the essential elements of Numeracy skills and objectives. "Almost all the interviewees are convinced of the necessity of basic numeracy skills as a prerequisite for promotion to first line of supervision level."[4] This latter finding confirms my own research findings regarding the reasons why adults participate in literacy programmes – to get promotion or job advancement. In this report the numeracy element of literacy skills seemed to emerge as more crucial for the operatives, supervisors and management who co-operated in this helpful study.

AnCO has also initiated other indirect and direct literacy activities.

Indirect Action

In 1976, The Curriculum Development section of AnCO surveyed the literacy problems which were being experienced by workers, and indirectly by trainers, in the AnCO training centres throughout Ireland. This investigation stimulated them to launch a research project to determine the literacy levels of jobs which trainees and apprentices were likely to undertake. This was a real and positive action by AnCO, which involved all the training centres and their personnel. It was also a sensitive operation, which created, in the centres, an awareness of the literacy problem and contributed to the development of a supportive atmosphere for future creative functional literacy initiatives by the Curriculum Development Section of AnCO.

Direct Action

AnCO, in co-operation with two Dublin based voluntary organisations (the Dublin Institute of Adult Education and the Dublin Catholic Social Services Organisation) started two pre-training courses which are directed towards either the unemployed youth (about 19 years of age) or a local community or unattached, unemployed youth. Each course continues for 10 weeks and has 10 participants. One of the courses (in the Dublin Institute of Adult Education) entails a direct literacy input of reading, writing, and arithmetic. The course is located in the Institute and thus has easy access to the literacy resources of this Institute. The literacy input during the second course is more indirect, less obvious, but nonetheless real and effective. It is integrated into the content and the teaching methodology of the course.

Both courses are being repeated every ten weeks. The participants in each course enter AnCO centres for more advanced training, or alternatively take up jobs which incorporate inservice or on-the-job training. It is hoped that similar projects will be launched in other parts of the country. These projects are still in their infancy, and have not yet been evaluated.

The Travelling People or Itinerants

There are about 12,000 travelling people in this country. Ninety-nine per cent of the adults (over 25 years) are illiterate, yet when there is a positive and supportive educational facility available, they seem to want to learn. About 95 per cent of the young adults, (14 to 25 years of age) are illiterate. In one year (1976/77) the number of these illiterates (14 to 27 years) was reduced by 10 per cent. A recent report states that over one third of these young adults can read and about a quarter can write. This is due, in great part, to the efforts of members of Settlement Committees, who undertook to tutor, on a one-to-one basis, the young adult itinerant. These committees are now firmly committed to the eradication of illiteracy among the travelling people.

There are now six industrial training centres for the young adult group. The training includes a literacy component. It is a vocational approach to literacy teaching. In the training centres, the young people learn first to be literate and numerate, but the greater part of the day, for the boys, is spent in learning metalwork and woodwork skills, mechanical skills, welding etc. The girls have courses in industrial machine-work, crafts of all kinds, cookery and dress-making, child care, hygiene and general preparation for marriage and motherhood. Eight more training centres will be established soon. The Combat Poverty Committee is financing one training project in Co. Clare. AnCO are involved in each of these projects. The local educational authorities also co-operate in these challenging enterprises.

In Bray, the trainees are being integrated with other socially disadvantaged young adults. Here an attempt is made to develop literacy and social integration among both the travelling people and the members of the local community. It is hoped that this latter project will receive some help from the E.E.C. Social Fund. A major problem for the literacy work among the travelling people is the very fact that they wander around. It is hoped to solve this problem by establishing these local training centres and concentrating on the training of the age group 14 to 25 years, i.e. those suitable for entry into employment.[5] Greater attention, too, will be given to numeracy problems among the travelling people. Literacy and numeracy still present major problems to them, however, which a national policy and campaign may not neglect.

Urgent Needs

The most urgent needs of tutors and organisers of adult literacy activities are the following:

(a) comprehensive training for their work.
(b) resources and materials relevant to adult literacy.
(c) appropriate tests to assess the literacy levels and needs of their learners.

The teaching of literacy to adults in Ireland is still in its infancy. Much has yet to be done to arouse government and public support for this work. A willingness to experiment in all areas of the work is absolutely necessary for the development and effectiveness of literacy schemes. Merely to copy what other countries are doing is not enough. Greater use must be made of educational technology, adult education research findings, and the life experiences of the learners themselves in designing, implementing and evaluating our work in this significant educational and truly human enterprise.

Since this paper was prepared, statements by the Minister of Education, John Boland T.D., made during the Adult Education Week, 1981, indicated that the Government acknowledged the existence of an adult literacy problem in Ireland and stressed that adult literacy must be given a high priority in the future development of the adult education provision in Ireland.

References

1. Ireland: Department of Education: *The Interim Report on Adult Education in Ireland*, The Stationery Office, 1969, Dublin.
2. Ireland: Department of Education: *Adult Education in Ireland:* Report of a Committee appointed by the Minister for Education, Dublin, The Stationery Office, 1973.
3. Singh, Sohan: *Learning to Read and Reading to Learn*, Teheran, International Institute for Adult Literacy Methods, Teheran, 1977.
4. O'Doherty, Dermot M.: *The Literacy Requirement of Occupations at Semi-skilled, Skilled, and First Line Supervisory Levels, in a sample of Irish Industries*, Unpublished thesis, Dept. of Sociology, University College, Galway, 1977.
5. Dwyer, Colette: *Report on the Education Needs of the Travelling People,* Dublin, 1975.

15. Problems Encountered in Education of Adult Illiterates in Third World Countries

Miriam and John Dean, Department of Library and Information Studies, University College, Dublin

The Extent of the Problem

The curiously transcendental term, Third World, appears to be generally accepted nowadays as an appropriate description for the new nations, most of which are economically or educationally deprived, or both. These nations frequently present a vast range of historical, cultural, religious, economic and linguistic differences, and while there are areas of similarity in respect of illiteracy, for the most part each country presents an idiosyncratic profile. Thus solutions to literacy problems must be purpose-built for each individual nation. The ideas that are to be discussed are of some variety and complexity and unfortunately less than justice can be accorded them in a brief presentation.

Consider for a moment the statistical aspects of the problem. A difficulty which confronts all investigators in the area of literacy studies relates to the inadequacy of statistical data. A host of factors contributes to the inaccuracy of information, e.g. doubts regarding definition, the unreliability of census administrators, shame felt by governments at admitting high illiteracy figures and so forth. However, certain conclusions may be drawn from the figures which do exist. During the decade from 1950 to 1960, the percentage of adult illiteracy in the world dropped from 44.3 per cent to 39.3 per cent, yet the actual number of illiterates increased from 700 million to 735 million.[1] The number of illiterates now are considerably in excess of this latter figure in spite of the enormous efforts made by numerous agencies, governmental and international, in implementing a whole range of schemes designed to promote literacy.

About 96 per cent of the total adult illiterates of the world live in the Third World countries. From data available we know that in Africa well over 60 per cent of the population is illiterate and in Asia, over 50 per cent. We know that the situation of the male is considerably better than that of the female throughout Third World countries, with a figure of 60 per cent illiteracy among women, as compared to 40 per cent among men.

Alas, the aphorism – educate the women and you educate a family – has only very limited application in the Third World today. Literacy programmes inevitably, in most areas, tend to be male orientated. This situation is well illustrated in the UNESCO document *Experimental world literacy programmes: a critical assessment.*[1] For example, in the Syrian Arab Republic eight literacy centres were set up solely for males in 1969/70; in the following year 1970/71, 23 centres were established for men and two for women, whilst in the last year of the project, 1971/72, there was a breakthrough and 52 centres were established of which 9 were for women. Thus whilst most concerned agencies have endeavoured to include women in programmes, progress has been slow.

The factors which inhibit the development of women educationally in the Third World are many and varied. For example, circumstances often militate against women being in the vicinity of available educational centres. It is customary in some societies for the males to work in the educationally well-endowed urban centres while the wife is left in the village to care for the children and till the fields. In other cases, where the women are urbanised, they frequently tend to forego their own opportunities in order to further the education of the family males in their search for advancement. Indeed, women themselves often tend to uphold those very cultural and economic patterns which restrict their own opportunities.

Thanks to various concerned agencies we have a better knowledge now of the extent of the problems of illiteracy among both men and women than we have ever had before. As a prelude to wider and more effective literacy programmes, difficulties associated with such undertakings are being more and more carefully scrutinised. Sometimes problems are so subtle as to be completely hidden from the uninitiated while others although self-evident have not in the past been sufficiently explored. It is encouraging to note that in the reports of UNESCO and other agencies, an increasingly critical attitude is adopted. Failure is identified no less clearly than success.

The Two Faces of Literacy

It is paradoxical that literacy itself creates so many problems for the illiterates; problems which have often gone unrecognised. An initial consideration of these problems is essential, since in some developing countries suspicion of literacy and fear of literacy serves to protect and perpetuate illiteracy. Literacy on the one hand is the key to greater freedom and greater social mobility, but on the other hand creates new bonds and may at the same time sow the seeds of disintegration and instability. Whether magico-religious, political or economic in origin, elitism inevitably undergoes some form of change when literacy strikes. The balanced traditional and essentially rural society, with its extended family relationships and long-standing pecking order, easily becomes eroded by change. Indeed, it may take several generations before this traditionalist society is superseded by some type of new order. As a consequence, it happens on occasions that some members of a particular society feel threatened with the onset of literacy and put up their barriers. They show their feelings either by active discouragement or more frequently by passive non-cooperation.

Examples of some of these feelings can perhaps best be taken from the areas of religion, myth and magic as practiced in some oral cultures. Both in the semi-literate societies, societies where literacy is in the hands of a selected elite, and in the completely illiterate community, the book encompasses not only the law, but also posseses in itself magical qualities. It is often quite difficult for the uninitiated to penetrate the circle of secrecy surrounding sacred and cherished texts. Foreigners are often unable to make much headway in this hidden society. For example, in parts of West Africa, such secrecy surrounds even the Koran itself, the magical qualities of which add to the power of its custodians in the local community.

The whole framework of a society is changed by the advent of literacy and concurrent technological expertise. One of the elements to be considered when introducing literacy to an oral culture is that one is probably sowing into a group-oriented community the seeds of individualism – and also the seeds of protest.

There is need for an awareness of the tremendous tensions engendered by fundamental changes in the role relationships of an entire society. New elites are created, sometimes superseding the old, sometimes integrating into the old order. Geographical boundaries expand as does knowledge itself. Desirable as these developments may be, especially in improving the living conditions, they can also cause a degree of psychological maladjustment hitherto unknown. Goody & Watt comment incisively upon the way in which literacy, while bringing to a community new knowledge, at the same time renders that community even more aware of its vast areas of ignorance:[2]

> The mere size of the (new) literary repertoire means that the proportion of the whole which any one individual knows must be infinitesimal in comparison with what obtains in oral cultures. Literate society merely by having no system of elimination, no 'structural amnesia', prevents the individual from participating fully in the total cultural tradition to anything like the extent possible in non-literate societies. (p. 340).

The function of socialisation of memory is of great importance both in the semi-literate and illiterate cultures, rationalising as it does the social events of the community into manageable segments; segments to be passed on from one generation to the next. Thus, we have two inter-dependent points, which can have a distressingly disorientating impact upon the establishment norms of a group, i.e. the psychological blow of not being able to know all things with the added disadvantage of not being able to forget. This may, indeed, be one of the reasons why neurosis is so extensive in newly literate societies.

A further point to be considered are the difficulties brought about in emergent countries by the proximity of literates and illiterates in the same society and even wthin the same family group. Literates normally remain in touch with their illiterate kin, and although the bonds may become progressively weaker, the illiterates will generally not be rejected as they are in metropolitan societies. However, where literacy is accompanied by urbanisation a subtle change in role relationships occurs between parents and child, particularly if an offspring returns to his village with visible and material signs of success. While some of the glory may be reflected upon the parents, there is often pain as well.[3]

Indeed, as more and more members of a society become literate, so that respect for the illiterates diminishes and they become figures of fun and sometimes of shame. Rose Kekedo comments:

> Much of the trouble in the village comes because the young educated people feel contempt for their older, wiser but uneducated, illiterate elders.[4]

As those in the metropolitan world know so well, where illiteracy is accompanied by a feeling of disgrace, so the work of the teacher is made more difficult. Thus, the success of literacy projects may well be endangered by patronage or insensitivity.

In concluding this section, it is stressed that inherent in the acquisition of literacy are hazards as well as rewards. Unless the dangers are understood, the benefits may not be acquired.

Organisational Problems

Some of the possible difficulties in the introduction of literacy programmes into traditional societies have been noted. It is now appropriate to consider the immediate organisational problems involved in the pre-planning, planning and implementation of literacy programmes. Governmental structures of Third World countries have as often as not been developed in an *ad hoc* fashion usually after a period of colonial rule. Many perpetuate the worst bureaucratic features of a superseded colonial regime. Administrative infrastructures tend to be weak and the negotiation of programmes with ministries is often fraught with difficulties; not the least of these being in the area of communication. There are in fact so many aid programmes competing for the attention of very few civil servants that only a proportion can in actual fact receive the consideration that is their due. One has also the feeling that literacy programmes do not merit the highest priority. Indeed, there is sometimes a feeling of embarrassment that a literacy problem should exist at all, and a wish that it would quietly go away, or at least remain unobserved. Disinterest, suspicion and lack of understanding result in inadequate planning, a failure to agree on objectives and a failure in collaboration between interested parties when a project eventually gets off the ground. Failures of this description have been noted *inter alia* in respect of the literacy projects conducted in Guinea and Algeria.[5]

Even when there is close collaboration between agency and government, no programme will succeed unless it it thoroughly researched on the spot to ensure that organisation at grass-roots level is effective. However well-intentioned a project, the organiser in Paris, New York or Canberra needs an input of local knowledge to achieve success. Timetabling difficulties in rural areas are particularly common, where classes often have to be arranged on a seasonal basis with allowances to be made for sowing, harvesting and so forth. Poor roads, inadequate transport, lack of space, unsuitable accommodation are further factors which constantly impede programmes, and even when everything appears to be shipshape, allowances will always have to be made for the unexpected; celebrations for the birth of a son; three-day wedding festivals; funerals; harvest festivals and similar occasions. In fact, flexibility without instability is probably the most valuable asset in the campaign team.

The Teachers and the Taught

The thoughtful selection of participants and experts will minimise organisational problems. This is no easy task. The choice of participants is particularly difficult. There are so many people to be taught and so few opportunities. The programme organiser is confronted with such overwhelming numbers that he will find it necessary to select those, the education of whom will benefit the greatest number in the shortest time. This implies that there is a tendency to select the fittest and brightest first, because they will contribute to productivity more quickly and hopefully most effectively. The weak, the undernourished and women, as mentioned previously, tend to be excluded. It is usual to include members of the community, who hold prestigious positions, in any literacy group. In fact, it is often the attitude of the community leader which will decide the success or failure of a project. If the community leader is committed to the programme, then other members of the community are also likely to be motivated in supporting the programme. This co-operation is possibly more effective in providing a willing audience than the most expensive array of audio-visual aids. Groups often reflect a considerable diversity of occupations and also span a wide age range.

This somewhat élitist approach would appear to be justified on the grounds that by taking the most able in the community the message will be spread more widely and more quickly than by any other method. However, in a few countries determined efforts are being made to improve the literacy situation of even those people who are not particularly highly motivated.

The choice of expert is as crucial to the success of any scheme as the choice of participants. Government agencies, philanthropic bodies and interested organisations have in the past exercised too little concern in the selection of experts with frequently disastrous consequences.[6] The situation has vastly improved of late, but the oversights and omissions indicated by Asheim are, from time to time, still encountered.

Programme Design

Programme design is often a most contentious area and has sparked a great deal of controversy among the educators. This rather competitive attitude, however, has its advantages since it has produced a reasonable variety of imaginative material and resulted in the discarding of quantities of inadequate and inappropriate material. Thus we have a number of approaches to programme planning and programme content.

It would appear logical that one of the first decisions to be made in planning a programme would relate to the language to be used in the campaign. Sometimes the choice of language is difficult. As a result of numerous factors, including colonial partitioning, a number of the emergent countries embrace a vast number of cultures with many different languages. For instance, in Papua New Guinea at least 700 vernacular languages have been recorded. In India the problem is enormous and as noted in the 1961 census, 1,549 separate languages or dialects are spoken. In Indonesia there are at least 50, and a similar number in countries such as Nigeria and Ghana. These are just a few examples of the many that could be given.

Once the task of choosing a language or range of languages has been accomplished then the planners may be confronted with the problem of selecting the appropriate orthography. This problem is particularly relevant to establish orthographies for languages which have no equivalents in the Indo-European family.

It may be appropriate at this juncture to refer to the difficulties encountered when introducing simple illustrative matter into a literacy programme. Such frustrations were experienced, for example, by the group working upon the Malagasy literacy programme.[7] Participants in the course experienced considerable difficulty in interpreting pictures and the assessors commented: "We thus find that the peasantry have never been taught to 'see pictures', anymore than they have been taught to read and calculate (p. 387)." One problem that can arise relates to the scale of an illustration. It has, sometimes, to be actually explained that the object which is depicted as being about two inches by two inches is, in fact, a representation of an object which is actually fifty feet by fifty feet. Similarly, elements of time are expressed in many different ways in different cultures across the world. Thus, differences in the *Weltanschauung* that exist between countries cannot always be adequately interpreted by the alien.

No mention has been made so far regarding programme content. This is an extremely difficult area. And clearly in the production of new packages, the relevance of the materials to the environment of the learner has been increasingly recognised in practice. Programmes which proceed too rapidly into the *terra incognita* of new technological structures may well cause unnecessary tensions among learners. Those which are initially based upon the learner's own experiences may be in the long run more successful.

Programme presentation too has undergone radical changes in recent years. Nowadays few postillions are being struck by lightning. Similarly the structure of a Latin grammar is no longer seen as the ultimate paradigm for all languages at all times.

Obviously the factors considered in programme development are infinitely more numerous, subtle and complex than has been indicated, but space precludes further elaboration.

Summing Up

In reviewing the issues that face the world in eradicating illiteracy, one can but be aghast at the formidable task ahead – a task that is becoming more and not less demanding. An analysis of the possible areas of failure indicates the immensity of the challenge presented.

In the first section it was noted how important it is for experts to be sensitive to nuance, and to appreciate the essentially individual nature of the cultural environment in which programmes are customarily conducted.

At the level of negotiation and planning it has been observed that in many cases collaboration between campaign organisers and governments has not always been forthcoming. The task imposed on the major executives responsible for literacy programme policy, is demanding in the extreme. It requires an understanding of the ideological and bureaucratic systems characteristic of recipient governments; a knowledge, moreover, which necessarily comprehends an appreciation of the loci of power within governments and areas of possible conflict.

Finally, it must be emphasised, that in spite of massive efforts, literacy projects in most parts of the world tend to be episodic rather than a dynamic component of each country's educational infrastructure. Problems are many, solutions few.

References and Bibliography

1. UNESCO. *Experimental world literacy programmes: a critical assessment.* Paris: UNESCO, 1976, (b).
2. Goody, J. and Watt, I. The consequences of literacy. In Gigliole, P.P. (Ed.) *Language and Social Content.* Harmondsworth: Penguin, 1972, p. 340.
3. Lloyd, P.C. (Ed.) *The new elites of tropical Africa.* London: Oxford University Press, 1966, p. 29.
4. Kekedo, R. Vernacular literacy. *Teacher: Journal of the Papua New Guinea Teachers' Association,* 1976, 1 (1).
5. UNESCO. *Experimental world literacy programmes: a critical assessment.* Paris: UNESCO, 1976, (b), pp. 17 and 47.
6. Asheim, L. *Librarianship in developing countries.* Urbana: University of Illinois Press, 1968. p. 88.
7. UNESCO. Practical guide to functional literacy. Paris: UNESCO, 1973, (a).
8. Goody, J. Uses of literacy in Northern Ghana. In J. Goody (Ed.) *Literacy in traditional societies.* Cambridge: University Press, 1968.
9. Meggitt, M. Uses of literacy in New Guinea and Melanesia. In J. Goody (Ed.) *Literacy in traditional societies.* Cambridge: University Press, 1968.

VI. LITERACY AND HISTORICAL PERSPECTIVES ON READING

16. A Poet's View of Reading

Seamus Heaney, Carysfort College, Dublin

The Oxford Dictionary of English Etymology has two entries for the word *read.* The first one is derived from Old English *reada*, and has now a technical sense meaning "the stomach of an animal" (and we might come back to that sense of the word later). But it is the second entry that concerns us here: "read, preterite and past participle, read(red) meant originally think, suppose, guess, discern the meaning of (chiefy in *read a riddle*, *a dream*);" and hence the next accretion of its sense – "inspect and interpret aloud or silently (signs representing speech); also intransitive. OE *raedan* = OFris, *reda,* OS. *radan* (Du. *raden* advise guess), OHG. ratan (G. *raten* guess, read (a riddle), advise), *ON rada* advise, plan, contrive, rule, explain, read.... The original senses of the German verb are those of taking or giving counsel, taking charge, controlling .... the sense of considering or explaining something secret or mysterious is common to several languages, but that of interpreting written symbols is peculiar to OE and ON...."

So long before the written symbol men have been reading, reading faces, reading fortunes, reading skies, reading entrails, "your face, my lord, is as a book where men may read strange matters," says Lady Macbeth to her husband, but obviously from the etymological evidence, from the spread of the word's tentacular roots, the sound and sense of read was planted among our Indo-European ancestors. And in this original sense, of considering and deriving meanings from the evidence of our senses, the illiterate are probably still better readers than the literate. Among primitive peoples and generally among those untouched by the Gutenburg revolution, the world itself is a system of hieroglyphs, some of which each member of the tribe can interpret. Illiterate man watched birds, watched animal tracks, watched the track of the sun and the moon, watched equinoxes and eclipses with the same unthinking attention as we now watch road signs, shop-signs, headlines, bus-signs. He deciphered the natural world into information and meanings. He translated, and in a way, reading is still a form of translation, a carrying over of sense from the visual world into the mental, a finding of equivalents for letters, a transference and mutation.

But there can be no reading in our sense without writing. We take these arts so much for granted now that we forget what a great creative act it was in the first place to invent this new language of silence which the alphabet implies. Some of the wonder of it is dramatised for me when I recall an old man who lived beside us when I was a youngster, a man who had hired out in hiring fairs from the age of 9 or 10, who lived in the only clay-floored, mud-walled house I ever knew and who thereby had the status of archaic man about him. The stones of his hearth were cobbled into the black packed earth, and his hearthstone was literally and obviously that, a large flag selected for its size, placed under the open chimney for its natural shape. He was small and bowed, he smelt of woodsmoke, he had altogether the tang of the remote past about him. But he also had sons in America and he would occasionally receive letters from them. He would then land into our house with the pages already a bit smudged from his pockets and his seasoned fingers, and present them to be uncoded, turned into speech by somebody with the gift. My mother would read the news aloud and the keenness, the almost animal alertness with which he attended, listening as much with his eyes as with his ears, is a sharp and tender human image for what the dictionary calls "interpreting aloud signs representing human speech", and a reminder that romantic elevations of the unlettered man, the noble savage, ignore too lightly the fundamental gifts of civilisation and education.

Something of that sense of wonder and gratitude for the invented symbols of the alphabet and the numerals is caught by Joseph Tomelty in his play *All Souls Night* where an old Co.

Down fisherman, embarrassed at having to put an X on his pension book has his hand guided by a girl and succeeds in tracing out his own signature. Then he goes on to muse over the few numbers she has written down for him in these terms: "And that's an O, round like a sail-ring or an eye of a herring; and that's a five, shaped like a cuphook in the dresser, and a six, like what a worm would ooze on the sand." That again is a beautiful piece of translation, transposing the symbols of learning into the substance of his own world. But it is a vivid illustration too of the otherness of the written, of its artificiality, its conventional nature, a reminder if we needed a reminder, of the considerable effort of memorisation and recognition called for before the pristine innocent eye can make sense of the printed page.

But of course the old man was eager to learn and had the gift of close observation naturally. He would represent the kind of pupil every teacher of reading wants to have. But in the next piece, the pupil is of a type that is probably more familiar. It is a poem by Richard Murphy about teaching a fourteen-year-old boy to read, a tinker boy, again with a whiff of the primitive hunting man about him, and again it dramatises very nicely the contrast between the skills of open road and open field and the skills of the study:

Fourteen years old, learning the alphabet,
He finds letters harder to catch than hares
Without a greyhound. Can't I give him a dog
To track them down, or put them in a cage?
He's caught in a trap, until I let him go,
Pinioned by "Don't you want to learn to read?"
"I'll be the same man whatever I do."

He looks at a page as a mule balks at a gap
From which a goat may hobble out and bleat.
His eyes jink from a sentence like flushed snipe
Escaping shot. A sharp word, and he'll mooch
Back to his piebald mare and bantam cock.
Our purpose is as tricky to retrieve
As mercury from a smashed thermometer.

"I'll not read any more." Should I give up?
His hands, long fingered as a Celtic scribe's,
Will grow callous, gathering sticks or scrap;
Exploring pockets of the horny drunk
Loiterers at the fairs, giving them lice.
A neighbour chuckles. "You can never tame
The wild duck: when his wings grow, he'll fly off."

If books resembled roads, he'd quickly read:
But they're small farms to him, fenced by the page,
Ploughed into lines, with letters drilled like oats:
A field of tasks he'll always be outside.
If words were bank notes, he would filch a wad;
If they were pheasants, they'd be in his pot
For breakfast, or if wrens he'd make them king.[1]

I suppose there are indeed those who think of the words they read as banknotes, who think of reading as an earning capacity, as primarily a utilitarian acquisition. Those advertisements for speed reading courses are set up to make us feel that reading is a form of piece work, almost; the more you can pack in in the shorter time, the bigger the returns. Reading becomes a form of raiding at most, a kind of minimal modern world survival kit at least. The faster you read, the farther you'll go. And of course there's a lot in this. As the man used to say to me on the road home from school, "What book are you in now, young Heaney?" You remember how at one time your progress and advance through the school was not marked out in classses but in books, the first book, the second book and so on. Your increasing knowledge was increasing power. But whatever book you were in, the advice was always tendered, "Stick at the books. The pen's a lot lighter than the spade." The books could translate you finally from the earth of physical labour to the heaven of education and redemption from physical work. And this barter power of reading is of course not to be ignored or neglected. But as a writer and a reader, I am perhaps more interested in words as pheasants or wrens than words as bank notes. As pheasants and wrens they stand for reading as an enhancing of the imagination, a pleasuring of the sympathies and intuitions and emotions that bind us together as feeling human beings rather than as economic units or registers on the social scale. For if reading is an act of translation, of carrying over from the symbol into the apprehension and understanding, it is also an act of carrying away, into the memory and imperceptibly into the personality. I would not go as far as my old headmaster, Michael McLaverty, the short story writer, used to go, who used to visit my classroom when I taught in English at an Intermediate school in Ballymurphy in Belfast. He had a vivid and infectious trust in the power of literature to refine and enrich a person's life, and when he visited me to give a pep talk to the classes, he used to conduct elaborate conversations with me, for them to remember and ponder. And one of his more arresting examples of how silk purses were made by the action of reading would always come like this: "Mr Heaney, when you see a photograph of a rugby team in the *Irish News,* can't you always tell by looking at their faces which of them read poetry?" To which I would faithfully and fallaciously reply, "Always."

But McLaverty was merely caricaturing a belief which we all have in the nurturing, humanising effect of imaginative writing and imaginative reading, and it is here where that first technical meaning of *read* that I found in the dictionary becomes relevant. For if we are successful in teaching that first ability to translate, we must surely proceed to nurse the ability to ruminate. If *read* is to mean the stomach of an animal, its *rumen*, in Latin, then I want it to be the stomach of a cow. Reading is the mind's cud, we might say, and the savour of reading experiences lingers and is refreshable and refreshing to the imagination. Again, if I might try to illustrate what I mean by anecdote and analogy. I have a friend, a singer, who goes for a couple of months to Donegal each summer. Now and again he sings in a bar at night, Irish songs, Scotch songs, cowboy songs, and each year when he comes back he gets requests for the old favourites. A couple of years ago a quiet man called James Big Ned asked him to sing again the one about the white horse. So my friend started the ballad about Belfast that begins

Red brick in the suburb, white horse on the wall
Italian marbles in the great city hall
O stranger from England, why stand you aghast
May the Lord in his mercy look down on Belfast.

But no, that was not what JBN was after. He racked his brains and tried out different tunes until he hit on the tune of that lovely lingering melody that some use for *The Bard of Armagh*, but which this man uses for *The Streets of Laredo*. And that was the song, *The Streets of Laredo*, about the young cowboy cut down in his prime, remorseful, tender, calling up on his companions to carry him to the churchyard, calling for roses to deaden the clods as they fall. But, of course, the song has no white horse in it anywhere. It's just that the melody and the atmosphere and melancholy feeling that he experienced while listening to the thing drifted and misted into this evocative image. Something in his own life and experience and emotional make-up was appeased by the white horse.

And that action of the song in the mind and life of that listener is analogous, I think, to the experience of reading imaginative literature, that literature that uses words to affect our feelings and to inveigle our experience of life into the experience of a fiction. It is an invisible action, it is an unquantifiable action, but it goes on at those levels of the mind which are to do with our emotional peace and understanding, those levels where words are not just counters, printed symbols, carriers of information but where they have become instinct with human attachments, with all the associations of a personal life.

References

1. Murphy, Richard. The Reading Lesson. In *Selected Poems*. London, Faber and Faber, 1979. Reprinted by kind permission of the publishers.

17. When the Theories and Practice Fail: the Search for the Beginning Reading Teacher in Revolutionary America

John W. Delonas, Lehigh Univerisity, Pennsylvania

The Problem

This paper, based on earlier research,[1] covers the impact of revolutionary demands for universal literacy upon traditional theory and practice, with special reference to female education. This paper is intended to show: (a) how contradictions in theory influenced the universal literacy goals; (b) that the traditional male teachers could not meet the new nationalistic reading demands; and (c) how the new free schools and new child-centred teaching produced a new and enduring profession – the female reading teacher.

Revolutionary Demands on Education

A colony on the edge of the "howling wilderness" had defeated England, but its chances of survival appeared slim with three European powers on its borders. American leaders realised that the people spoke many varieties of English dialect, German, etc. They looked to a system of education that would unite the people in the common bond of standard English and the sharing of a common patriotism through a uniform reading program. This uniting-through-reading would help the new nation survive. The leaders trusted in the newspapers to protect the public from political corruption. President Jefferson believed that informed citizens could keep the reins on a government. "In a republic, every one hath to act a part, and he should be able to read and write, and to justify how he votes."[2] Intelligent citizens knew from their classical readings that a high rate of literacy marched with victorious armies. They correlated the decay of ancient civilisations with a decline in literacy. So, American plans of education envisioned free schooling to all citizens sufficient to make them understand the newspapers.[3,4]

Those equal laws our citizens demand,
Justice requires that they should understand;
From public schools shall general knowledge flow,
For 'tis the people's sacred right – to know . . .[5]

Traditional Theories and Plans for Education

The demands of the revolution put a strain on the old educational theories.[6,7,8] Earlier theorists fell because their ideas were oriented to the private tutoring of a gentleman's son. For revolutionary Americans, only universal education would permit every citizen 'to act his part' in the management of his country. Contrary to egalitarian purposes, the old philosophers were anti-female in their ideas. While Rousseau's writings gave new impetus for the re-education of male youth, he insisted that most little girls did not like to learn to read, and preferred to use the needle so as to adorn themselves.[6] Erasmus' support of local schools was popular, but not his condemnation of dame schools.[7] Even Americans who produced influential plans of schooling had given little thought to beginning reading and female education.[8,9,10]

If universal literacy was to be realised, it would have to depend on women and on 'initiatory' schools. Yet, female education barely existed. As for schools, the model of American Education might best be described as an aristocratic head (university) upon a plebian (common school) frame. *The Universal Asylum*[11] compared beginning education with college thus: "the laying of a foundation which is despicable, without the superstructure.' Francis Hopkinson would describe the primary school as a 'first entrance to the Garden of Human Knowledge which leads only through a long barren path, producing little else but a few useful and necessary herbs.'[12] Magazines on both sides of the ocean liked to quote Dr. Samuel Johnson as to the unimportance and misery of initiatory schooling.[13,14]

Thus, neither the theories nor the popular prejudices were helpful in promoting universal literacy through the medium of schools. The women who would be the agents linking nationalism with instruction were, themselves, largely uneducated. It would take over a century to fully overcome these deficits.

The Practice of Schooling

Where educated male teachers were available, they often taught beginning English reading according to the rules of Latin. Supervision of curriculum was almost unknown. Many schools were lacking in materials for teaching reading. The type of textbook (often the Bible) available generally determined the type of instruction offered.[15]

Chambers described the typical school as a 'little, wretched hovel.'[16] Brutality and rebellion could make teaching a risky undertaking.

> Time was, a tutor was obey'd and fear'd
> 'Till youth grew fit for office: now alas!
> Let him but chide a child of seven years old,
> And the brat flings the tablets at his head –
> You hasten to his father, and complain:
> And redress? aha! old Bumbrusher,
> You see my boy here can defend himself,
> So touch him at your peril . . . .[11]

The poorest children were often not educated at all. 'Latin' was the key to schools that prepared the better classes for the learned professions. Livingston and Smith proposed to exclude Catholics from a planned New York College.[17] Parents of one religious persuasion would not send their children to a schoolmaster of another faith.

Although the hornbook was the traditional beginning text for boys, little girls may have learned to read by stitching samplers at home.[18, 19] When a boy could pronounce English words of three syllables length, he was sent to the Latin Grammar School. Girls' schooling terminated when they could read the primer through.[15] Female instruction, the *American Museum* noted, has been left to chance, or not conducted beyond the lowest forms.[20]

Rush reported that the chief objection to public schools had always been their mischievous influence upon young morals.[21] A new school in Philadelphia was praised for its moral calibre:

> Who would not chuse *(sic)* rather to see his son in such a seminary, than in any obscure corner, under immoral . . . Drunkards, professed Gamesters, concealed Irish Papists, or others . . .[22]

For moral reasons, many parents refused to give their children any schooling at all, unless it was a local and orthodox school they could keep an eye on.[23] Chambers pleaded for the discovery of some method which would supersede the necessity of going to school to learn to read where tender infants learned bad habits.[16]

Schoolmasters seem to have been of indifferent quality and ill-suited for the job. Colonial communities sometimes had to resort to indentured servants for teachers. In 1776, the *Maryland Journal* advertised that a ship had just arrived from Belfast and Cork, and enumerated among its products for sale "various Irish commodities, among which are school masters, beef, pork, and potatoes."[24, 25]

After the revolution, numerous plans were launched to reform the schools, but there was a practical defect that the reformers could not overcome – the shortage of male teachers of good character and training. So long as women were brought up un-educated, society had to make do with transient male teachers.

> Many of our inferior schools, which, so far as the heart is concerned, are as important as colleges, are kept by men of no breeding, and many of them, by men infamous for the most detestable vices . . . . Will it be denied, that before the war, it was a frequent practice

> for gentlemen to purchase convicts, who had been transported for their crimes, and employ them as private tutors in their families.[26]

Many parents, it was noted, care little what sort of persons they employ, or what methods they pursue. They are indifferent to both. Cheapness of education is all the cry,[27] Teachers were no better in England, being in Macaulay's words: "the refuse of other callings – discarded servants, or ruined tradesmen; who cannot do a sum of three, who would not be able to write a common letter . . ."[28] Even the schoolmasters' advocacy of the classical languages worked against them for the Ancients held teaching children in low esteem.[29]

The root of the problem for males was that teaching little children was not considered to be a man's employment. *The Independent Reflector* noted that "the masters are such as have been graduated from their colleges and for want of estates, *stoop* to this employment."[23] The poem, *Progress of Dullness*[30] depicts the country schoolmaster at his worst.

> Few months now past, he sees with pain
> His purse as empty as his brain
> His father leaves him then to fate,
> And throws him off, as useless weight;
> But gives him good advice, to teach
> A school at first, and then to preach . . .
> Next see our youth at school appear,
> Procur'd for forty pounds a year,
> His ragged regiment round assemble,
> Taught, not to read, but fear and tremble . . .
> He tries, with ease and unconcern,
> To teach what ne'er himself could learn; . . .
> The year is done, he takes his leave;
> The children smile; the parents grieve;
> And seek again, their school to keep,
> One just as good, and just as cheap.

American towns needed teachers recruited from their own citizenry; of high moral and orthodox character; docile in temperament, who looked on teaching as a career – and who would work cheaply. The need could be supplied by women, once the female education issue was decided. Mott reported that the female education issue was the one subject that all the magazines wrote on.[31] Knox feared that vice and vanity would soon corrupt virgin innocence in female seminaries. Women, he added, needed the protection of the father's bosom.[32] Another article warned that the results of education would be buying expensive clothes and becoming chatterboxes.[33] *The Retailer* saw education for the upper class women and then only as a re-creation in leisure. But he did praise the development of female academies.[34] Begrudgingly, the male prohibitions against higher education gave way. A marvelous lady, "Sylvia" argued for female education thus:

> So, Mr Reformer, you are concerned for the education of the fair sex, are you? Your servant Sir – your servant Mr. Leander . . . by your manner of writing about ideas – it is probable that you and your intimate friend are fresh . . . from the university, big with a sense of your own importance, each of you having there exercised your mind, sufficiently to discover (and shrewd is the discovery) that our sex, as they never go, and never ought to go, to college, have no business with . . . Newton, or Locke . . . nor a good serious book on controversial divinity.[35]

Apparently, the prevailing educational technique for teaching girls to read was stitching ABC's on a sampler, for it struck a sensitive nerve in Sylvia:

> Upon your peril do not tell Philander in your next letter, that I had better have been using my *needle*. . . . Pray Mr. Leander, which makes the most uncouth appearance, "A doctor in petticoats," or a scribbling, perfumed, he-she creature in the dress of your sex? . . . why should we be utterly debarred from some particular studies merely because

> some gentlemen think their sex have an exclusive right to them. . . .[35]

Despite magazine warnings that reading novels would make women extravagant and useless;[36] or that an attachment for books would keep her from matrimony;[26] journals increasingly came to support female education.[20, 21] Women's colleges were incorporated with the authority to confer degrees. Educated women were at last moving towards taking over the job of initial teaching and giving elementary schools a cadre of respectable, career-oriented professionals.

The Reform

New theories and plans that included the notion of "affectional" discipline evolved during this time. *The Academician* reported the spread of the ideas of Pestalozzi in England and Ireland.[37] Pestalozzi declared that the art of instruction could be managed so that children would enjoy it. Love could be expressed in a graded classroom where the children's age was to determine what was to be taught and how.[38] Periodicals encouraged young ladies to qualify themselves for teaching infant schools by entering seminaries where modern applications of Pestalozzi were imparted.[39] Women's teaching roles in Dame schools, charity and Sunday schools had given them the experience which allowed them to step forward in response to the nationalistic demands for universal literacy at the primary level.

Conclusions

The essence of the old theories rested in the quality of the parenting relationship between the child and the tutor. Rousseau and Locke saw the tutor dedicating his life to his pupil. But this affection-bond and life-dedication was not found in many of the male teachers teaching 40 or more children in single classrooms. Prescribed social roles tended to work against males becoming professionals in beginning reading instruction. The theorists never anticipated an Industrial Revolution or national defense requirements of a literate public to handle technology or safeguard a republic.

The emergence of the female teacher, graded primary schools, and the printing explosion (penny papers, steam press, cheap reading series, free religious tracts) produced a close relationship between school practice and new theories of Utilitarianism, moralism, Pestalozzi, and Philanthropy. The graded reading series that were pouring off the presses helped make the idea of age grouping feasible. The new dictionaries made real the patriots' demands for a unified language and consistent spelling. And age-grouping and technology required a school building of many classrooms and departments. Children, so divided, were easier for female teachers to manage. The economics of the new schools required scientific training in specialised areas for teachers as well as a permanent cadre of professional supervisors – because public taxes to educate the public's children, had to be accounted for.

But, when patriotism called for universal literacy through a free initiatory school system, it was women in their despised Dame schools or voluntary Sunday Schools, who were in the best position to meet nationalistic requirements.

British Utilitarianism maintained that it was wasteful not to educate girls. Research showed that literate factory workers produced more than illiterate workers.[28] Many educated women worked in the mills – why not in the schools? Pestalozzian and Philanthropic concepts encouraged love and tenderness in teaching babes to read. Women had been educating their children for centuries. Now masculine institutions were recognising that fact. The dedication of mothering easily shifted to the dedication of the "schoolmarm". One poet recognised the selflessness that has always characterised women involved with children:

From the lofty summit of her mind looks down,
Rich without gold, and great without renown.[40]

References and Bibliography

1. Delonas, J. The Struggle for Reading as Seen in American Magazines. Unpublished doctoral dissertation, Michigan State University, 1976.
2. Eliot, J. On Education. *The Boston Magazine*, 1784, 4, 238-9.
3. Lee, G. *Crusade Against Ignorance: Thomas Jefferson on Education.* New York: Teachers College Press, Columbia University, 1961.
4. Welsh, T. On Education. *The Boston Magazine*, 1784, 3, 176-8.
5. Philo. Public Schools. *The American Museum*, 1792, 6, 296-8.
6. Boyd, W. *The Minor Educational Writings of Jean Jacques Rousseau.* New York: Teachers' College Press, Columbia University, 1962.
7. Gay, P. *John Locke on Education.* New York: Teachers College Press, Columbia University, 1964.
8. Woodard, W. *Desiderius Erasmus Concerning the Aim and Method of Education.* New York: Teachers College Press, Columbia University, 1964.
9. Best, J. *Benjamin Franklin on Education.* New York: Teachers' College Press, Columbia University, 1962.
10. Kiefer, M. *American Children through their Books.* Philadelphia, Pa.: University of Pennsylvania Press, 1948.
11. Wilson, M. On a Liberal Education: Some new Remarks from Experience. *Universal Asylum and Columbian Magazine*, 1787, 2, 263-7.
12. Hopkinson, F. Extraordinary Dream. *The Pennsylvania Magazine, or American Monthly Museum*, 1775, 1, 15-9.
13. Franklin Primer. *North American Review*, 1829, 4, 489-503.
14. Remarks on the Principal Roots of the Latin Tongue. *Gentlemen's Magazine*, 1826, 6, 514-517.
15. Lamport, H. A History of the Teaching of Beginning Reading. Unpublished doctoral dissertation, University of Chicago, 1935.
16. Chambers, J. Elements of Orthography: An Attempt to Form a Complete System of Letters. *Universal Asylum and Columbian Magazine*, 1791, 10, 225-8.
17. Remarks on our Intended College. *The Independent Reflector*, 1753, 3, 67-8.
18. Meriwether, C. *Our Colonial Curriculum*, 1607-1776. Washington, D.C.: Central Publishing Co., 1907.
19. Reeder, R. *The Historical Development of School Readers and of Methods in Teaching Reading.* New York: Macmillan Co., 1900.
20. Magaw, S. An Address Delivered to the Young Ladies' Academy at Philadelphia. *The American Museum*, 1788, 1, 25-8.
21. Rush, B. Thoughts on Female Education. *Universal Asylum and Columbian Magazine*, 1790, 4, 210-214.
22. Account of the College and Academy at Philadelphia. *The American Magazine*, and Monthly Chronicle for the British Colonies, 1758, 10, 633-4.
23. Letter from Philadelphia. *The Independent Reflector*, 1753, 11, 204-5.

24. Hofstadter, R. *Anti-Intellectualism in American Life.* New York: Random House, 1963.
25. Wright, L. *The Cultural Life of the American Colonies, 1607-1763.* New York: Harper and Row, 1957.
26. Education – the Practice of Employing Low and Vicious Characters in Schools Reprobated. *The American Magazine*, 1788, 3, 210-6.
27. Academician, No. IX. *The Academician*, 1818, 7, 113-115.
28. Altick, R. *The English Common Reader.* Chicago, Illinois: The University of Chicago Press, 1957.
29. Mathews, M. *Teaching to Read Historically Considered.* Chicago, Illinois: University of Chicago Press, 1966.
30. Trumbull, J. The Rare Adventures of Tom Brainless. *The American Magazine*, 1788, 1, 117-119.
31. Mott, F. *A History of American Magazines, I: 1741-1850.* Cambridge, Massachusetts: Harvard University Press, 1966.
32. Knox, V. On the Literary Education of Women. *The Universal Magazine*, 1781, 1, 42-3.
33. Witherspoon, J. A Series of Letters on Education, Letter IV. *The Pennsylvania Magazine or, American Monthly Museum*, 1775, 9, 399-405.
34. Retailer. *Universal Asylum and Columbian Magazine*, 1789, 4, 252.
35. Sylvia. To the 'Young Gentleman' whose Letter on Female Education was Published last Month. *The Royal American Magazine*, 1774, 5, 178-9.
36. Philaleths. On the Practice of Reading Novels and Romances, Letter III. *The United States Magazine*, 1794, 6, 140-2.
37. Fellenberg's School. *The Academician*, 1819, 7, 320-5.
38. Greene, M. *The Public School and the Private Vision.* New York: Random House, 1965.
39. Butler, V. Education as Revealed by New England Newspapers Prior to 1850. Unpublished doctoral dissertation, Temple University, 1935.
40. On Female Education. *The Royal American Magazine*, 1774, 1, 9-10.
41. Nye, R. *The Cultural Life of the New Nation, 1776-1830.* New York: Harper and Row, 1960.

18. Developments in English Reading in the Irish National Schools, 1937-77

John Coolahan, Education Department, University College, Dublin

Introduction

This paper is best seen as a continuation of the historical background to the teaching of English reading in Irish National Schools which was delivered at the annual conference of the Reading Association of Ireland in 1976.[1] On that occasion the approaches towards English reading during three eras of diverse policy covering the period from circa 1872 to 1937 were explored. It is now proposed to survey developments during the last four decades, a period with which many readers have some familiarity and of which many have considerable first-hand experience.

Political and Administration Background

The year 1937 saw the promulgation of a new constitution which set forth the relative status of the Irish and English languages in the Irish State in the following manner:

1. The Irish language as the national language is the first official language.
2. The English language is recognised as a second official language.
3. Provision may, however, be made by law for the exclusive use of either of the said languages for any one or more

> official purposes, either throughout the state or in any part thereof.[2]

As was the case in earlier periods, socio-political attitudes exercised very direct influence on curricular policy. Differing interpretations of the national objective of the restoration of the language continued to cause confusion and conflict and this affected the position of English in the education system. On the one hand there was evidence of impatience that after fifteen years of Free State curricular policy the position of Irish as vernacular had not made greater progress. On the other hand some people felt that educational considerations were being undermined for political and ideological reasons and that the prevailing policy towards Irish and English was having deleterious consequences for children's educational development.

The position of English in the schools cannot be adequately understood without some awareness of the climate of thought which existed. Some events of the early forties can serve as a barometer of that climate and illustrate contrasting attitudes. In March, 1941, the Department of Education issued a circular to schools the contents and phraseology of which projected the two languages as being engaged in a conflict or battle situation in the schools. The circular posited the vulnerable position of an Ireland "isolated between two English-speaking countries which are pouring on us an ocean of English speech and thought."[3] The school-children were urged that they should not form "as it were, soldiers on the side of English in the war it is waging against the Irish Language."[4] It was recommended that schools become "the fortresses of the Gael in the fierce struggle."[5] Indeed the Minister for Education, Mr. Derrig, saw no compromise possible in this battle of the languages and stated in Dáil Éireann in May 1943 that Irish could not be saved "without urging a most intense war against English, and against nature itself for the life of the language."[6]

This intense projection at official level of a conflict situation between Irish and English was likely to have affected attitudes towards English in the classrooms and to have impeded whole-hearted initiatives towards improving English teaching in schools. With the main thrust of educational policy aimed at improving the position of Irish it may be that inspectors and teachers concentrated less on the complexities of English teaching and may not have directed their optimum energies and skills in that direction. This surmise gains some substantiation from discussions with teachers, and from research studies in later years. Macnamara in his study of bilingualism in Irish National Schools, noted that inspectors tended to rate highly those teachers whose pupils achieved a high standard in Irish or in Arithmetic, but not in English, and he suggested that such trends may have "resulted in a relative lack of concern in the majority of teachers."[7] Greaney and Kellaghan in a survey they carried out in 1968 found that teachers did not perceive English reading as being a major source of pupil difficulty.[8] In a more recent study of teaching styles for English reading Greaney gave it as his opinion that teachers did not regard English as a subject worthy of serious consideration.[9] The absence of more comprehensive evidence prevents us coming to firm conclusions about attitudes to English in the schools but pointers exist which indicate that English had a relatively low status and that official policy statements were a contributory factor in this.

One of the groups which was becoming increasingly dissatisfied with official policy in the early years of the period under review was the Irish National Teachers' Organisation (INTO). As a result of a questionnaire among its members the INTO issued an interim report in 1939 on teaching through Irish in the infant school, followed in 1941 by the publication of a full report on the use of Irish as a teaching medium to children whose home language was English. In the first report it was concluded that "the majority of infant teachers are opposed to using Irish as a sole medium of instruction when English is the home language."[10] In the final report the majority of teachers asserted that the benefit from instruction in school subjects through the medium of Irish was not equal to the benefit from instruction through the medium of English.[11] These comments by the teachers met with no favourable responses in official policy. In fact the main departmental initiative in these years was that in opposition to the INTO, the Department of Education in 1943 made the primary certificate a compulsory examination for children in sixth class of the primary school. The examination was confined to written papers in Irish, English and Arithmetic. The examination in English consisted of an essay together with comprehension and some grammar questions on a piece of unseen prose. Official statistics did not give a breakdown of success rates in the individual subjects. The general pass rates, however, improved from 71.6 per cent in 1944 to 81.3 per cent in 1954, with pass rates for subsequent years ranging from 77 to 82 per cent.[12]

Appraisals and Proposals

The end of the Second World War heralded in a period of reforming zeal in the educational systems of many European countries. In line with this general desire for change the INTO produced its *Plan for Education* in 1947. It sought many wide-scale reforms in the Irish education system and particularly in school curricula. The report deprecated much of the English reading in school. It made a special plea to the Department to involve itself in the provision of school libraries, drawing attention "to the fact that our Department of Education has made no organised attempt to provide money or books for school libraries."[13]

This report gave rise to no new departures in Irish educational policy. However, in 1950 the Inter-Party Government established a Council of Education, which had been frequently called for. It was to be an advisory body and its first formal task was to report on:

(a) The function of the primary school;

(b) The curriculum to be pursued in the primary school.

The fact that the Council's mind was to be concentrated on the national school curriculum might suggest that fundamental re-appraisals would take place. However, when it reported in 1954 the position of English in the school was given scant attention and any recommendations were rather platitudinous. A majority of the Council did recommend that English should be made a compulsory subject for one half-hour daily in Infant class in English-speaking districts.[14] Speech training was urged to be the sole purpose of English in the Infant school and reading urged to be postponed to Standard 1. The report urged that greater use should be made of silent reading in the senior classes. The report had nothing to say on approaches to teaching reading, on the quality or type of textbooks in use, on the time allotted to the subject throughout the school, on the dearth of school libraries or supplemental reading materials. There was no analysis of children's reading though detective and cowboy stories were frowned upon while it was held that comics provided "a special and grave problem" and that "the moral tone of a great many calls for the utmost vigilance on the part of parents."[15] No specific advice on English reading was forthcoming and the general comments concluded by remarking, "The aim, however, should be to direct the child's natural interest in reading better literature, which can be most suitably supplied by history and stories from history."[16] In thus dealing with English reading in the schools one considers that a valuable opportunity for authoritative and in-depth appraisal by the Council of the existing position was lost and no informed guidelines were available to affect policies or programmes in reading.

Programme and Method

What then were the programme and approach to English reading in the schools? The programme required that English be taught as an obligatory subject from Second class upwards and accordingly deal only with these classes. The requirements for English reading were stated in terse and concise terms. For instance, in the senior classes, it comprised one sentence: "To read intelligently a suitable reader or storybook."[17] The approach to the teaching of English reading in Irish schools continued to rely on the use of basal classroom readers. The *Notes for Teachers* were based on the assumption of a common reader with the teacher conducting the procedure for the whole class as a unit. A most notable feature of the Notes, however, was their altogether unchanged character from those issued in 1933. The suggested manner of conducting the reading lessons followed the pattern laid down then. As a consequence when statements (such as the following) reappear in the 1959 edition – "The practice of silent reading cannot be said to have had a fair trial in our schools" – one wonders if this was genuinely the case or whether it was that the authorities did not consider it worthwhile re-assessing whether the existing situation was still the same as it had been in 1933.

The annual Reports of the Department are not informative of the situation in the schools when they do make any reference to the position of English reading. Yet, as the following quotation from the Report of 1956-57 would suggest, silent reading was making some limited headway:

> Déantar roinnt taoi-léitheóireachta ins na h-árdranganna agus is iad téascsleabhair na scoile a usáidtear de ghnáth. Ceapann cuid de na cigirí nach ndéantar dóthain dí ar chor ar bith; agus deireann cuid eile nach mbíonn cumas léitheóireachta sách maith i gcoitinne ag daltaí na n-árdrang féin i gcuid de na scoil-eanna chun an taoi-léitheóireacht a chleach-tadh go foirleathan.[18]

In a research study in 1963 Jordan claimed that the method usually followed in Irish classrooms was the traditional and, in his view, wasteful one of reading orally around the class.[19] Gorman in a study of 1968 found that many schools taught reading through the spelling method and used very little supplementary material.[20]

Textbooks

The class reader held a place of central importance in the child's mastery of reading and introduction to literature. The one basic text was taken at a pace directed by the teacher and was used to cover a whole year's work for pupils of all levels of ability in the class. The Department of Education retained the right to sanction or approve the textbooks used in the schools. The format, content and general presentation of textbooks tended to follow a set pattern over the years. Short topic lessons were interspersed with short adapted stories and occasional poems. In line with a standard curriculum for all types and sizes of National Schools the textbooks tried to establish a common denominator of theme and vocabulary with the consequence that they contained much that was foreign to the experience of children in different sub-cultural groups. The criticism of textbooks by the Tuairim Report in 1961 may have been too harsh when it stated: "The standard of most of the approved textbooks is deplorable. They are badly written, fatuous and shoddily produced."[21] Yet, it is true that many of the textbooks were rather stilted, lacked humour and provided little by way of stimulation to reading. As late as 1969 the Teachers' Study Group reported that "the teacher himself was confined in his choice of class reader to a limited number of textbooks which were generally found to be uninteresting and poorly illustrated."[22]

The lack of state or local authority funding for books other than very inadequate grants for free books to necessitous children tended to reinforce the narrow choice of books. For instance, the grant made available in 1954 was £4,925 with 479,487 pupils on roll; in 1964 it was £3,730 with 490,168 pupils on roll; in 1974 it amounted to £86,659 with 512,461 pupils on roll.[23] Thus, for most of the period the grants were piteously small and more than a few teachers exercised personal charity in providing basic textbooks for children from economically deprived homes. A tradition of "handing on" textbooks was a further deterrent against changing the textbooks in use in the schools. The use of a basal textbook for the whole class tended to discourage individual reading approaches. Kellaghan and Gorman, pointing to the disadvantages of a heavy reliance on single class-books, remarked:

> From an early age the child should learn how to use a wide range of books, how to be selective and critical, even sceptical – and above all he should learn to exercise his judgment. This we can hardly hope for if a child's experience of books is confined to a single textbook, however good.[24]

Library Facilities

Irish schools were very badly served in the provision of school libraries for most of the period. The Department of Education did not accept responsibility in the matter but, in the *Rules for National Schools* which it issued, managers were exhorted as follows:

> The Minister desires to urge upon the Managers the desirability of a small library for each school.[25]

No concerted initiative was taken by managers along these lines. When some library facilities were provided it was usually as a result of individual teachers' and local librarians' personal *ad hoc* arrangement.

It was not until 1963 that the Department of Education involved itself by providing a basic core of reference books to schools, valued at £32 per school, regardless of school size. In that same year, 1963, the Investment in Education team in its survey of school facilities found that 52 per cent of schools had some kind of library.[26] In another survey conducted in 1967 by Kellaghan and Gorman, it was calculated that 76 per cent of schools had some form of library. However, they found that the number of books available was quite limited, ranging from 0.6 of a book per pupil in city and rural schools, to one book per child in town schools.[27] Local authorities have become more involved with library provision to schools over the past decade and improved departmental grants have also helped to make libraries and supplementary reading a more normal feature of school life. For instance, in 1968 a scheme was drawn up in conjunction with the Department of Education whereby Dublin library authorities provided library facilities in National schools, and now all Dublin schools have some library provision. Other local authorities work schemes in their areas.

Standards Attained and Time Allotted

One of the difficulties in satisfactorily establishing the English reading standards of pupils was the lack of standarised attainment tests for Irish schools. In the 1960s a number of such tests devised for Irish conditions became available. In recent years considerable advances have been made in the provision of appropriate testing instruments which are likely to prove of great value for teachers in establishing standards of performance and in diagnosing weaknesses in reading skills. Despite the dearth of specially devised tests, efforts were made to establish some guidelines with regard to the comparative performance of Irish children's reading standards with their English peers. From his research conducted in 1961 Macnamara found that Irish children in English-speaking districts were about seventeen months behind the "English age" as measured for their counterparts in Kent.[28] Under the auspices of the Teachers' Study Group, McGee and Kelly conducted a survey in 1964 comparing English reading comprehension standards of Dublin schoolchildren with studies of their English peers. The 1964 survey indicated a difference of approximately twenty-six months in reading age between Dublin children and children of similar ages in England and Wales. A follow-up study in 1969 reflected no significant improvement, while a further study in 1974 has revealed an improvement in reading comprehension by the Dublin pupils, resulting in a lessening of the gap.[29]

One regrets the absence of further evidence, but the indications were that the standards in English reading among Irish pupils were considerably below their English counterparts. That a gap should exist was to be expected in view of the fact that the Irish children had to master two languages. Differing and often very emotional points of view exist on the tolerance level of the gap in standard because of other political and educational objectives. Yet, as a pure matter of fact, the gap was wide and disquieting to many. While many causes could be adduced for this, it is worth noting that the policy of the Department often resulted in an intentional down-grading of English, and English was practically banned from the Infant school.

A number of studies endeavoured to assess the time devoted to English in the National schools. The Investment in Education team reported that out of an approximate 22.5 hour teaching week, 10 were devoted to language, of which 3.5 were allocated to English. Macnamara found that 42 per cent of the school week was devoted to Irish and 22 per cent to English. English children had more than twice as much exposure to English at school as the Irish pupils. Such factors, coupled with the official policy referred to earlier, the attitudes of the inspectorate and some teachers, the lack of fresh initiatives and guidelines on the teaching of the subject, and paucity in the provision of books, all combined to cast a shadow over the position of English in the schools.

"Fresh Fields and Pastures New"?

Though the promotion of English lacked whole-hearted endeavour, this did not mean that individuals failed to accomplish some excellent work in the teaching of English. Some teachers and inspectors prompted by their own interest made valuable initiatives in the teaching of reading. The efforts of such people had a rippling effect and contributed to the changed climate of thought which led to the publication of a new curriculum for national schools in 1971. This provided official endorsement of new trends and developments.

The New Curriculum reflected a major change in the curricular policy of the state. Included in this was a much altered attitude towards English, and more especially, English reading. As the curriculum rightly commented, "The importance of reading efficiency in child-centred education cannot be over-stated."[30] A varied, adaptable programme was suggested for different stages of children's development. Teachers were encouraged to employ a wide battery of teaching strategies and aids in helping children's reading progress. More refined diagnostic attitudes and modes of discrimination were applied to reading skills.

English was now accepted as an important element of school life from the Infant school upwards. The set oral reading lesson was to be largely abandoned and it was stated:

> This will involve the use within one class of different books or of different parts of the same book; the guiding principle is that the reading difficulty of the material in use must match as closely as possible the reading ability of the pupil.[31]

Variety of task was stressed in such quotations as the following:

> The period devoted to the teaching of reading *per se* will vary in purpose and in length at each level of development. At one time or another, it will include, singly or in combination, work on oral reading, silent reading, word-recognition, word-analysis and synthesis, explanation and discussion of reading matter,

> preparation for work-book activity or other writing based on what is read, or work in spelling.[32]

If the aims of the new programme were to be fulfilled it was also urged that "wide use of class and school libraries, works of fiction, poetry, encyclopedias, etc."[33] was to be incorporated in school work.

The more fresh, interesting and varied approaches to English reading have, in the opinion of teachers, led to significant improvements in English reading. In a national survey conducted by the INTO in 1976 approximately 80 per cent of respondents felt that the standard of English reading had improved during the first five years of the operation of the new curriculum.[34] A number of other developments over the last decade would seem to have had a cumulative effect in placing English reading as a central pre-occupation of the educational system. The operation of summer and in-service courses; the provision of teaching centres and study networks; the establishing of courses in remedial reading; the appointment of reading specialists in the training colleges; the greater availability of library facilities and supplemental readers; the wider dissemination of pedagogical techniques and aids for reading; the development of appropriate attainment and diagnostic reading tests; the establishment of the Reading Association of Ireland, aimed at focusing interest in research and skills in reading – would suggest a brighter future and improved opportunities for English reading to the greater enrichment and personal development of the children in the schools.

Concluding Comments

Reflecting back on the forty years under review, one is struck by the long period in which no fundamental re-appraisal with regard to English took place. The lack of fresh thinking and initiatives towards English reading gave it an aura of staleness and routine. The traditional textbooks and traditional methods contributed to a lack of vitality. As a grounding in English and introduction to English literature, the process was frequently dull and uninspiring. For many children it was the only formal introduction they were to get, bearing in mind that as late as 1962, one out of every three children left formal education at the National School level and less than half of these had obtained the Primary School Certificate.[35] For much of the period emigration rates were high, with England as the predominant destination for emigrants. It is difficult to feel complacent about the levels of competence in English with which they were equipped. Perhaps the basic underlying problem was the failure to come to grips with and clearly articulate educational policies with regard to language in a bilingual state. Different groups held different beliefs, assumptions and allegiances which were overlaid with a good deal of vagueness and ambiguity. There was a reluctance to move towards definition and clarification of relative positions. Things were allowed to drift, as the State vacillated in terms of establishing or coming to grips with its cultural identity. Perhaps it was necessary for time to elapse before definition could take place. The problem of the place of English, the colonial language, but yet the home language of the majority of the people in the State, set in juxtaposition to the official language which the State set out to revive and restore was a difficult and intriguing one. The Irish experience of this problem is of considerable interest and import to general educational and cultural history. One suggests that the relative position of the two languages was closely interwoven with the problem of cultural identity in the state – a debate which is unfolding but is as yet unresolved.

References

1. Coolahan, John. "Three Eras in Reading, in V. Greaney (Ed.) *Studies in Reading*. Dublin. Ed. Co. 1978, pp 12-26.
2. *Constitution of Ireland*, Article 8.
3. *Revival of Irish: What Children Can Do?* Circular to Manager and Principals of National Schools, issued by Department of Education, March 1941 p. 7.
4. Ibid.
5. Ibid.
6. Dáil Éireann, *Parliamentary Debates*, XC, 105, 176, 12, 13 May 1943.
7. Macnamara, John. *Bilingualism and Primary Education, A Study of Irish Experience*. Edinburgh University Press, 1966, p. 125.

8. Greaney, V. and Kellaghan, T. "Cognitive and Personality Factors associated with the class placement of pupils." *Irish Journal of Education*, 1972, pp. 93-104, p. 101.
9. Greaney, V. *An Experimental Investigation of Individualised Reading,* Unpublished M. Litt. Thesis, Trinity College, 1969, p. 16.
10. INTO, *The Uses of Irish as a Teaching Medium to Children Whose Language is English.* Dublin, 1941, p. 19.
11. Ibid. p. 28.
12. Annual Reports of Department of Education.
13. INTO, *A Plan for Education*, Dublin, INTO, p. 72.
14. Department of Education *Report of Council of Education,* Dublin, 1954, p.2
(Note: In 1948 the Department had permitted English as an optional subject in infant study for one half hour per day.)
15. Ibid., p. 172.
16. Ibid.
17. *Programme of Primary Instruction.* Dublin, The Stationery Office, 1956, p. 9.
18. *Report of the Department of Education* for 1956-1957, p.9. A rough translation reads: "Some silent reading is done in the senior classes and it is the school textbooks that are usually read. Some inspectors feel that not enough of it is done at all while others report that the standard of reading in general is not sufficiently high among even the senior pupils to have silent reading practised on a general basis".
19. Jordan, M.J. "*The Leisure Time Reading of Dublin School Children*", unpublished M.A. thesis, U.C.D., 1963, p. 97.
20. Gorman, W.G. *The Construction and Standardisation of a Verbal Reasoning Test for age range 10 years – 0 mths. to 12 years – 11 mths. in an Irish Population.* Unpublished Ph.D. thesis, U.C.D., 1968, pp. 15, 16.
21. Tuairim: *Irish Education*, Tuairim, London, 1961, p.5.
22. Teachers' Study Group, *Reports on the Draft Curriculum for Primary Schools*, Dublin, 1969, p. 14.
23. Annual Reports of Department of Education.
24. Kellaghan, T. and Gorman L. "A Survey of Teaching Aids in Irish Primary Schools", *Irish Journal of Education*, 1968, II, pp. 32-40, p. 34.
25. Department of Education *Rules for National Schools*, Dublin, The Stationery Office, 1965, par. 20, p. 14.
26. *Investment in Education*, Dublin, The Stationery Office, 1966, Table 9.21, p. 250.
27. Kellaghan and Gorman, op. cit. pp. 34, 35.
28. Macnamara, J. op. cit. p. 134.
29. Patrick McGee, "An Examination of Trends in Reading Achievement in Dublin over a Ten-Year Period" In V. Greaney (Ed.) *Studies in Reading*, Dublin, Educational Company, 1977, p. 33.
30. Department of Education, *Primary School Curriculum: Teachers' Handbook, Part 1.* Dublin, The Stationery Office, 1971, p. 106.

31. Ibid., p. 108.
32. Ibid., p. 93.
33. Ibid., p. 95.
34. Report of Education Committee of INTO on "The New Curriculum", *An Múinteoir Náisiunta*, Vol. 20, No. 7, September, 1976, p. 21.
35. *Investment in Education*, Dublin, 1966, Vol. I., pp. 139-141.

NOTES ON CONTRIBUTORS

William W. Anderson is Professor at the School of Education and Professional Studies, Shippensburg State College, Shippensburg, Pennsylvania, U.S.A.

Rev. Liam Carey is Lecturer at the Department of Adult and Community Education St. Patrick's College, Maynooth, Ireland.

John Coolahan is Lecturer in Education at the Department of Education, University College, Belfield, Dublin.

John Dean is Professor and Head of the Department of Library and Information Studies, University College, Dublin.

John Delonas is Professor of Education at Lehigh University, Pennsylvania.

Sean N. Farren is Lecturer in Education at the Education Centre, The New University of Ulster.

James T. Fleming is Professor at the Department of Educational Psychology and Statistics, State University of New York at Albany, New York.

Patricia Fontes is a Research Fellow at the Educational Research Centre, St. Patrick's College, Dublin.

Seamus Heaney is a poet and former Lecturer in English at Our Lady of Mercy College of Education, Carysfort Park, Blackrock, Co. Dublin. He now teaches at Harvard University.

Thomas Kellaghan is Director of the Educational Research Centre, St. Patrick's College, Dublin.

George Livingstone is Lecturer in Education at Hamilton College of Education, Scotland.

Michael Lynch is a school teacher in Tralee, Co. Kerry and holds a doctorate in Educational Psychology from University College, Dublin.

Fergus McBride is a Senior Lecturer at Moray House College of Education, Edinburgh.

Anne McKenna is Lecturer in Developmental Psychology at the Department of Psychology, University College, Dublin 4.

Joanne B. Nurss is Professor of Early Childhood Education at Georgia State University, Atlanta, Georgia, U.S.A.

Fred W. Ohnmacht is Professor and Chairman of the Department of Reading at the State University of New York at Albany, New York, U.S.A.

Ellen O'Leary is Lecturer at the Department of Education, University College, Dublin

Jessie Reid is Lecturer in Education at the University of Edinburgh.

Desmond Swan is Professor and Head of the Education Department, University College, Dublin.

Gerard M. Ryan is a psychologist with the Eastern Health Board, Dublin.

General Index

Coláiste Oideachais Mhuire Gan Smál
Luimneach